THE
VISITATION
HANDBOOK

FOR THE CUSTODIAL PARENT

Your Complete Guide to Parenting Apart

———

BRETTE MCWHORTER SEMBER
ATTORNEY AT LAW

D1576271

SPHINX® PUBLISHING
AN IMPRINT OF SOURCEBOOKS, INC.®
NAPERVILLE, ILLINOIS

First Edition, 2002

Published by: **Sphinx® Publishing, An Imprint of Sourcebooks, Inc.®**

<u>Naperville Office</u>
P.O. Box 4410
Naperville, Illinois 60567-4410
630-961-3900
Fax: 630-961-2168
http://www.sourcebooks.com
http://www.SphinxLegal.com

This publication is designed to provide accurate and authoritative information in regard to the subject matter covered. It is sold with the understanding that the publisher is not engaged in rendering legal, accounting, or other professional service. If legal advice or other expert assistance is required, the services of a competent professional person should be sought.

From a Declaration of Principles Jointly Adopted by a Committee of the American Bar Association and a Committee of Publishers and Associations

This product is not a substitute for legal advice.

Disclaimer required by Texas statutes.

Library of Congress Cataloging-in-Publication Data
Sember, Brette McWhorter, 1968-
    The visitation handbook : your complete guide to parenting apart / Brette McWhorter Sember.-- 1st ed.
        p. cm.
Includes index.
    ISBN 1-57248-192-7
    1. Divorced parents--United States. 2. Parent and child--United States. 3. Visitation rights (Domestic relations)--United States. I. Title.
    HQ759.915 .S456 2002
    306.85'6--dc21
                                                    2002017670

Printed and bound in the United States of America.
VHG Paperback — 10 9 8 7 6 5 4 3 2 1

For Terry, Quinne and Zayne

I would like to thank the children I worked with when I was practicing law, who led me to the deeply personal insights behind this book. Having worked so closely with them and having been so involved in their lives, I felt deeply compelled to write a book that would help their parents improve their situations. I offer my deepest respect and admiration for the judges and court personnel who handle these cases with such care and empathy.

Thanks also go out to my agent Sheree Bykofsky for her support and help; my parents, Thomas and Kathleen McWhorter for everything they do; my friends and sounding boards, Belle Wong and Brigitte Thompson; Joanne Wilton, MSW, for discussing the initial concept of this book with me; my husband and children, who put up with my hours in front of a computer; and the dogs who warm my feet and heart as I write.

TABLE OF CONTENTS

PREFACE

This book is two books in one; one side of the book for each of the parents who have gone through a divorce or separation. In most divorces or separations, the child lives primarily with one parent (the custodial parent) and spends time with the other parent (non-custodial parent). Both parents are equally important to the child.

This book has two separate parts and is what is called a "flip book." It has two parts to fully address the unique concerns, situations, emotions and difficulties faced by parents in each role. While the advice, examples and problems described for each type of parent may be different, the underlying message is the same for each: focus on your child, learn to cope with dealing with the other parent, and move forward in your life as a parent.

The book is written in two parts, each with its own cover, chapters and appendices because both parents in a child's life are equally important and because parents in each role face different problems and concerns. This book is a *symbol* of that.

Many books offer psychological perspectives on co-parenting, single parenthood, and life after divorce. This isn't one of them. Written by a divorce and family attorney, the book gives you a practical roadmap for living with visitation. The author worked in family court, representing children and parents. She saw the problems families face as they try to navigate through visitation and the changes it brings. This book is filled with practical tips that are based on her experience with real families.

There are lots of books that tell you how to get yourself and your child through the actual divorce, but none that tell you how you are going to live in this new situation created by the divorce or separation. It is difficult to adjust to a completely new life and it is difficult to continue to manage visitation and parenting through the years following a divorce or separation. Living with this new plan is like nothing else you have done before. Many families have trouble coping with the challenges visitation brings. They end up returning to court where they let the court work out their disputes and make changes to their schedule. Some families end up in a revolving door syndrome, where they are constantly returning to court on a regular basis. This constant uncertainty takes its toll on the parents—but especially on the child.

This book will help you avoid the revolving door. It is a guide for you to use now, but also for you to return to again and again as your child grows, your situation changes, and new challenges and obstacles arise.

It is important to note that both males and females take on both of the parenting roles discussed in this book. If you are a non-custodial mother or a custodial father, you might sometimes feel you are in an unusual role. This book is here to help all divorced parents regardless of their gender and regardless of which role they are in.

This book is also unique in that it is written for parents in both the United States and Canada. The problems concerning living with visitation are universal and are not specific to certain states or countries. Each half of the book contains an extensive appendix that will help you find resources, support groups, books and web sites that can help you. A separate appendix has been created with Canadian resources for Canadian parents.

The book carefully refers to "the other parent" throughout the book. This is a purposeful attempt to get you to think of him or her in this way. He or she is your child's other parent and it is important for your child's health and well-being that you respect and accept this. Try to avoid thinking of him or her as your ex, former spouse, etc. Keep your focus on your joint parenting responsibilities.

This wording is also used because many parents never marry each other. It is common for people to become a couple, have a child and then separate. This book is written for you whether you have been married or not, divorced or separated, are currently in the midst of divorcing or separating, or even if you and the other parent never even had any long term relationship at all but did create a child together.

The book generally refers to "your child." Obviously many people have more than one child. If you have more than one child, apply the advice given to all of your children. When the text refers to "your child" this generally includes children and teens of all ages. If a situation is different for teens, it will be specifically mentioned. The book will help you understand the different reactions children will have at different ages and also discusses how sibling relationships are affected by visitation.

Both parents are needed in a child's life. You are to be commended for wanting to focus on your child's needs. This book will help you through the difficulties visitation brings and will help you and your child make the most of your situation.

This unique flip book is written both for you and the other parent. After you have read the side written for you, you might also want to read the side that is written for the other parent so that you can look at things from his or her perspective. Share this book with the other parent.

Refer to this book when you are first adjusting to living with visitation, and also in the future. Problems and concerns are certain to come up down the road that you cannot now anticipate. Keep this book as a reference guide to use for those future situations.

NOTE

If your relationship with the other parent was abusive or if you feel now that you could be in danger from the other parent, this book is not designed for you. If you feel you are in danger, you should speak to your attorney or get help from a shelter for battered spouses. If you feel your child is in danger from the other parent, you should contact your attorney and your local department of family and children's services.

INTRODUCTION

You have faced the end of your marriage or relationship, been through the courts or mediation, and now your child is living primarily with you and spending time with the other parent. The custody and visitation arrangement you have may not be ideal in your mind. Now that you are through the craziness of the legal process and the difficult emotions that accompany it, your first order of business has to be taking everything that has happened in your life, in court and inside you, and just letting it settle in. You'll have to work through it all somehow for your own sanity.

There are many books and resources available to help you heal the pain of divorce. This is not one of them. This book is designed to help you manage, understand and maximize your parenting time. The book is written not by a psychologist or social worker, but by an attorney who has spent much time in court and in the homes of families facing and working through visitation. The author worked one on one with parents and children, many of them on a daily basis, as they struggled though the unraveling and reformation of their families. Some families were able to make their new situation work for them, but many more could not. These were the families who returned to court again and again as one or both of the parents continued to have problems living with the new arrangement.

Many families get caught in a revolving door, returning every few months to court to try once again to get something changed, when what really needs to change is their behavior and attitudes. This book offers practical, to-the-point solutions for the problems that you as a custodial parent are facing or about to face. If you can follow the advice in this book, you can avoid the family court revolving door syndrome.

The book is designed to help you through the confusing, upsetting, and sometimes hurtful process of being the parent who primarily resides with the child. No matter what has led you to this point, you are your child's parent and the role you play in his or her life is incredibly important. Your child has two parents and needs to be part of both of your lives.

You may feel constrained by the schedule you have to follow; you may find that it isn't completely convenient for you; you probably feel as if it is not entirely fair. You may also have reservations about the other parent's abilities or behavior. Despite all of that, it is up to you to help your child cope with the new arrangement as well as find a way for you to live with the arrangement you have. As the parent who spends the most time with your child, it is up to you to set the tone for how the new arrangement will be handled. It is up to you to make sure that the time you have with your child is the best it can be and that your child gets the benefits of visitation. This book contains pointers and tips to help you make the most of what you have, to help your child cope with the schedule, and continue to love and have a good relationship with the other parent. It is based on the author's experiences working with families that have gone through the same process you are now going through.

This book will discuss what you can expect from your child, yourself, the other parent, as well as other people in your life and your child's life with regard to the parenting schedule and visitation. The book focuses on how to manage the schedule as a practical matter, how to cope with it on an emotional level, how to help your child cope with it, and how to use it to benefit both of you. Each chapter deals with specific problems that come up during visitation and also addresses the different problems that come with children of different ages.

The advice is based on the author's first hand, up close experiences as a divorce and family attorney and mediator. The author's years of experience working as a Law Guardian for children, who are the subject of custody and visitation cases, brings the unique perspective of one who has watched the divorce process through the eyes of those children.

Many parents walk out of the courthouse with an order giving them residential custody with visitation to the other parent and a feeling that they have won. You have not won anything. You might have walked out of the courthouse feeling you got most of what you wanted, but that the other parent scored some victories as well. You must get all these thoughts out of your head. There are no winners and no victories. There is only the road ahead. You have to accept that whatever the judge decided or you agreed to is now how you will live your life. You must focus on helping your child deal with the arrangement and on making the arrangement as easy to live with as possible for both of you. This book will help you do just that.

How to Use This Book

Read this book and pay careful attention to the chapters that speak to your immediate concerns or problems. Keep the book handy and consult it as you experience new problems and different stages.

The book is designed to be your guidebook through the maze of being the custodial parent and coping with visitation. Many parents resolve their custody cases through settlement or a trial, head out to live with their parenting plan and end up back in the courtroom within a year because of practical problems with visitation. These problems can stem from any of the parties—the non-custodial parent, you, and even the child. Problems can include things such as a child not wanting to go on visitation, a custodial parent who tries to avoid visitation, and even disagreements over things like the child's laundry or homework. Visitation completely rearranges the lives of everyone involved. An adjustment period is necessary. Many families do not make it through the adjustment period without having to seek legal intervention. This book will help you with that difficult adjustment and steer you away from the pitfalls that bring so many families back through the courtroom door.

What This Book Cannot Do

What this book cannot do is change the facts of your situation. If you are certain that the parenting plan you have is not in the best interest of your child or is completely incompatible with your schedule, you need to contact an attorney or deal with the issue in mediation. Should you ever become concerned that your child is being physically or mentally abused, you need to take immediate action and contact your local police department or child protection agency.

Visitation is nothing more than a schedule that organizes everyone's time. It is not a decree that one of you is a bad or unimportant parent and that the other one is the better parent or has more clout with regard to the child. It is merely a time management tool. Learning how to make the most of what you have will help your child be healthy, feel loved and will bring you sanity. You can make visitation a wonderful part of your child's life while maintaining an equally wonderful relationship with your child yourself. Making the best of this situation is the best thing you will ever do for your child.

1

FACING REALITY

Now that the dust has cleared and you know what kind of arrangement you are going to have to live with, it's time to face reality. First, you need to completely understand what the schedule is and what rights you have. Next, you'll need to take a look at what that really means for you and your child. While it may be hard to adjust to your new life, you will find that there are many bright spots in it. This chapter will help you get a grip on your life and help you see what you have to smile about.

Understanding Terms

Now that you have residential or legal custody, you might not be entirely sure what rights it gives you. First, you need to read the judge's order or your settlement agreement carefully. These are some of the possible custody and visitation arrangements you might have:

Joint Custody with Visitation. You and the other parent share joint custody, with the child residing with you and visiting with the other parent. Joint custody means you are supposed to make decisions together about the child, such as where he or she goes to school, whether to have medical procedures done, etc. Joint custodians are expected to be able to communicate with each other. You, as the person the child lives with, leave as is *residential custody*. The other parent has visitation according to a schedule or when you both agree to it.

Sole Custody and Visitation. In this arrangement, you have sole custody and the other parent has visitation. This means the child lives primarily with you, and that you make most of the decisions about the child and are not required to get the other parent's input. The other parent has visitation at set times or at times as agreed upon.

Shared Custody. In this scenario, the child splits his or her time between you and the other parent equally. Both of you are responsible for making decisions about the child. Neither is considered to be the residential parent.

If you aren't sure which type of arrangement you have, call your attorney or mediator for help in understanding the wording in your judgment or order.

The most important thing to remember about the different arrangements is that they are just words. Your child is still your child. Your child is still the other parent's child as well. No one can take that away from either of you. Learn what arrangement you have and then FORGET IT. Your focus should be on your relationship with your child, not on a phrase and how it makes you feel, how it makes the other parent feel, or how other people react to it.

Changing the Schedule

If you have sole custody, or you share joint custody with the other parent, the child will have your home as his or her home base or residence. The other parent will have the right to see your child at the times outlined in your court order or judgment. What many parents do not realize is that you are not required to stick to the schedule set in the order or judgment. You and the other parent can agree to arrange visitation at any other times, change the times that are scheduled by the court, have the child spend less time with the other parent or basically make any adjustments you want to. However, you must both agree to any change. You must be certain that you can either trust the other parent to stick to the changes you agree to, or you need to get it in writing so that you have proof of the agreement in case there is ever a problem.

A parenting plan is not something that is set in stone and should be something that changes as the child and parents change. What works for a one year old will not work when the child is in kindergarten or in high school. You and the other parent should view the parenting plan or visitation schedule as a guideline, not as a hard and set law. See Chapter 6 for more about communicating with the other parent.

Don't Get Hung Up on Words

You should not focus on the word "visitation." When you and the other parent lived in the same house, you were parents together, period. You may have spent more time with your child or the other parent may have. It is important that you both continue to be parents and that your child continues to see you both as his or her parents.

Parents do not "visit" with their children. Parents *live* with their children. This is what you will both now be doing, except you will be doing it in different homes and at different times. In fact, many attorneys, mediators and judges are moving away from this poor choice of words and are now talking about "parenting time access," "parenting plans," and "parenting schedules." Try using these words because they will make your child feel more comfortable and will also make the other parent feel more comfortable. Try to see past the words to what is at the heart of the matter: your child. The other parent is much more than a "visitor" to your child.

Things Won't Be the Same

Now that you have digested the legal terms and gotten past them, you need to face another big mental challenge. Nothing in your life will ever be the same. That statement may seem to be huge, unfair and unbearable, but it is true. Your relationship with your child's other parent did not work and you have parted. You are living apart and this means that in order for your child to receive the benefit of being loved and supported by both parents, all three of you now must make changes and concessions to adapt to this new way of life.

Just because a situation is different, does not mean it can't be as good—or better—than the previous situation. Think about how unhappy everyone was when the relationship was coming apart. It was not a healthy situation for your child or for anyone else. You got out because you knew this. You now have the chance to build your own life and make your own way. In order to include your child in this and make sure the other parent is included in your child's life, you will have to make arrangements to do so. This means that you will have to make some concessions. The situation will not always meet your ideal.

Look at the Other Side

Just because your child will be spending more time with you does not make you the parenting "god" so to speak. It is very important that you recognize that both parents are important. You cannot change the other parent, you cannot change his or her behavior, and you cannot stop your child from loving him or her. You can find a way to accept that your child has two parents who are equally important in his or her life.

Your child has and needs to continue to have two parents who can, on some level, work together as parents. You may have divorced or separated from the other parent, but for the rest of your lives you will be parents together. You've got to accept this and find a way to make it work. You need to take a step back and view the situation from the other parents' point of view. He or she feels stripped of his or her parenting rights. A judge or an agreement has essentially pushed him or her aside and given you more time with your child. This must hurt. He or she feels afraid, cheated and lost, whether you believe he or she has a right to feel this way. Many times non-custodial parents react to this by being mean, being hurtful or by withdrawing. Think about how you would feel if you were to switch positions. You would feel the same way. Whether you believe it is right or are happy about it, your child needs to continue to have a relationship with the other parent. Your job is to make sure that happens. This is part of the responsibility of being the residential parent. You must push aside all the bad feelings you have about the other parent. In order for your child to grow up feeling loved, healthy and secure, you must make sure that you make room in your child's life for the other parent.

"Why am I responsible for his or her relationship with my child?" you are asking. Because this is what is best for your child. You love your child so much that you want to give him or her the world, right? Well, this is really and truly what your child needs. You need to not only make sure your child continues to be close to you, but that there is a closeness with the other parent. Your relationship with, and resentment, anger, hurt, and tangled emotions about the other parent must remain separate from this.

Let Go of Anger and Blame

You and the other parent broke up because you fought, were unhappy or blamed each other for things. Thankfully, that scenario is over. You don't need to live with anger on a daily basis now. You are certainly going to continue to feel some anger, and you probably have lots of things to blame the other parent for, but it does not need to be a central part of your life now.

If you continue to focus your anger (no matter how well justified it may be) and blame, you are never going to be able to get past it and find happiness on your own. If you are always angry, there is no way you can carry this burden without having it affect your child. As difficult as the divorce or separation has been for you, it has been at least a hundred times more difficult for your child.

Everything that has happened has been magnified through your child's eyes, increased by total or partial incomprehension, and heavily laced with emotional insecurity and fear. Whenever you are angry when you are with your child, he or she unconsciously interprets some or all of that anger as being directed towards him or her. Think about this. Every time you are angry, your child assumes it is because of him or her. Your anger has a very strong effect.

To continue to have a successful relationship with your child, you have to be able to mentally and emotionally focus. Anger is going to get in the way. You need some space in your head and your heart to make a plan for how you are going to parent from now on. If you are angry, you are using a lot of energy and effort for your anger.

Remind yourself that the other parent is NOT worth all this effort and angst. Now, none of this means that you aren't going to experience anger in the future. It is most assured that you and the other parent will continue to push each other's buttons. The two of you have had a lot of practice at it and it has become a habit. You're going to have to steer through these situations in the months ahead. If you haul along baggage from the past, it is just going to be harder to manage.

You are also experiencing a lot of hurt and loss. Some things have happened that you didn't deserve and you may have been rejected or insulted. Take the time to grieve for what you have lost, to feel the pain that is associated with a relationship ending and then face the future. You may never completely get over what has happened, in a way the pain will always be a part of you, but you have to move forward now.

Resolve to make a fresh start with the following tips:

➤ Decide that the past is the past. It's over and you're letting go of it.
➤ Let yourself go through the natural grieving process associated with divorce or separation. It's OK to be sad for a while.
➤ Let go of your anger. It isn't helping you.
➤ Think about your future and make plans for what you want and what you will do.
➤ Take it slow. A fresh start is a gradual process. Give yourself time.
➤ Focus on the love you have for your child. This is what really matters.
➤ Look at things positively. Think about the time you do have with your child.
➤ Make your child the center of your world instead of your problems with the other parent.
➤ Smile! A whole new world is ahead of you.

You aren't perfect and, of course, you're going to slip up, but try very hard to focus on your child and not on your failed relationship with the other parent. You have a lot of work ahead.

Dealing with Loss

When the divorce or custody case was initially decided, you might have felt in some ways like you were the winner. After all, you have more time to spend with your child than the other parent. As you move forward in your situation, you might also start to feel as if you have lost something. You don't get to spend every day with your child and there are moments in his or her life you won't be present for. Some custodial parents feel a deep sense of loss about this.

Your child will now be away from you for periods of time, while before you were together every day. You probably resent the other parent for taking this time away from you. You need to realize that although you will not have as much time with your child as you did before, you still have more time than the other parent and you must not begrudge him or her the time that is allotted. Keep in mind that your loss is your child's gain. He or she needs to have time with the other parent. The time you have with your child is your time alone without any interference from the other parent. Enjoy what you have.

Respect Visitation

You've just read that you need to focus on your child. Your first thought may have been that you have been doing exactly that and it is part of the reason you needed to end the relationship and obtain custody. You need to continue to focus on your child and you need to remember that you absolutely must give visitation a priority. You're probably relieved not to have to spend time with the other parent, but your child certainly doesn't feel that way. Make sure you respect the visitation time that is scheduled or agreed upon and don't put up roadblocks.

This also means that you must have a positive and encouraging attitude about visitation. You need to convey to your child that you *want* him or her to spend time with the other parent. You must demonstrate that you respect this new, separate relationship your child has with the other parent. You should not convey feelings of resentment or anger about visitation.

Focusing on your child also means that you need to re-evaluate your entire situation. When you see your ex, you may see red, but you need to turn your eyes to your child and make him or her the focus of the situation. When you fail to respect or allow visitation, you are not punishing the other parent; you are punishing your child. It is also important that you make time to spend with your child. It is easy for this to get lost in the craziness of everyday life. Make a point to spend real, one-on-one time with your child on a regular basis and give him or her your full attention.

As you first experience being a custodial or residential parent, it will be difficult to juggle all the changes you are facing. You feel afraid, overwhelmed by being alone, lost, scared, abandoned and relieved. Visitation may feel like a disruption or an intrusion. It will get easier and you will find a new routine that incorporates the visitation schedule into your normal life. Your child will come to adjust to it as well, and you will become comfortable with your new family routine.

Here are some ways to help you focus on your child:

➤ Think about the time you have, not the time you are missing.
➤ Don't let your child see or feel the anger you have towards the other parent.
➤ Make visitation a priority because it is important for your child.
➤ Encourage visitation between your child and the other parent.
➤ Show respect for your child's relationship with the other parent.
➤ Encourage your child to have contact with the other parent when they are apart.
➤ Consider how your child is feeling and think about how you can help.
➤ Arrange to spend one-on-one time with your child when you can give him or her your undivided attention.

2

YOUR CHANGING RELATIONSHIP WITH YOUR CHILD

If you haven't realized it yet, your relationship with your child changes as a result of the divorce or separation. Your child probably grew up being parented by two parents. You and the other parent made decisions together, or at least you were both involved in some way. Now your child is parented by two parents who are in separate homes and each is probably parenting without the other's input. Your child has gone from getting a kind of average of the two of you to getting the two extremes. This is a huge change for everyone.

Your child is dealing with one or possibly two new residences, as well as a schedule that could be very confusing and hard to adjust to. All of these changes have had an effect on your child and may cause him or her to act differently. You are learning to be a single parent, with no back up from the other parent. You will find that you act differently because of this.

You have also gone through some rough times. You have gone through the break up of a relationship, a court proceeding and all the deep emotional difficulties these two very stressful situations have brought you. You're probably not who you used to be either. You can see that you and your child both have changed, so it makes sense that your relationship has changed and will continue to change.

The Effects of Divorce

Much research has been conducted to study the effects of divorce on children. While there are some basic truths these studies reveal, the fact is that each child is unique and may react differently from other children. Read about some of the common effects, but keep in mind that your child may not be typical.

In general, look for these common reactions to divorce:
- ➤ sadness and grief;
- ➤ anger;
- ➤ desire to place blame (on parents and on themselves);
- ➤ fear of abandonment and loss;
- ➤ divided loyalties (wanting to be loyal to both parents, even when this is impossible);
- ➤ denial;
- ➤ school and social problems;
- ➤ withdrawal;
- ➤ low self esteem;
- ➤ inability to trust people or form bonds; and/or,
- ➤ physical symptoms such as stomachaches and headaches.

Reactions by Ages

Expect preschool children to blame themselves and possibly to regress or go backwards a bit in their development. School age children experience worries about the future and are at a higher risk of depression. These children also often "act out." Teenagers frequently take sides in a divorce and experience financial worries because of it. They also feel negatively about marriage as an institution and try to physically and emotionally distance themselves from home and home life. See Chapter 13 for more information about how reactions differ by age.

Gender Differences

Girls are likely to react by trying to make connections with males or by trying to bring male influences into the mother's home. Girls, in general, try to be perfect to prevent future problems. Boys are likely to react by trying to fill their father's shoes by acting as the man of the house at the mother's home. Boys try to suppress their feelings of great sadness and may become more aggressive. Low self esteem is a problem.

For more information about children's reactions, refer to the resources listed in Appendix B at the end of this book.

Riding the Ups and Downs

One of the most important things to expect about the adjustment you and your child are making is that there will be ups and downs. You may have a terrific week together and feel as if you are getting back on track, and then you may have a few bad weeks. You need to remember that adjusting to the situation is a lengthy process. Nothing that happens is going to be set in stone—good times and bad times are to be expected. Everything is going to be in flux for quite a while.

When you are experiencing good times, enjoy them. Let yourself relax and be happy. Your child might return from visitation without you having a fight with the other parent or your child might be thrilled to see you. You might spend some time together and find yourselves being comfortable and feeling really connected. If you have a day like this, soak it up.

Do not expect it to last and do not be disappointed when something happens to bring the good times to an end. If your child has a tantrum and says, "I hate you," tells you he or she would rather live with the other parent, or complains that you don't do things the same way as the other parent, don't see it as the end of the world. All children have short attention spans, all children have tantrums, and no parent is perfect. Don't expect perfection from yourself or your child and you won't be disappointed. You must also remember that as a parent, it is not your job to make sure your child is happy every moment and that he or she has everything he or she wants. It is your job to make and enforce rules, give and receive love openly, and be willing to communicate. You are not a playmate or someone whose job it is to please your child. Read Chapter 4 for more about establishing rules.

Try to see everything that happens as part of the big picture. One bad day does not seem so terrible in the context of a month or a year. Keep your perspective and remember that nothing that happens is the end of the world.

You also need to understand that even as you and your child become accustomed to the new arrangement, changes will happen in your lives that can send things into the air again. You might meet someone new that you care about or your child might get a job or start playing on a sports team. You and your child are always changing and your times together will be constantly changing as well.

Dealing with the Bad Times

Just as you can't have good times all the time, neither can you have bad times that never end. You may have some very difficult periods of time to get through, but they will pass. The beauty of children is that they are always growing and changing.

If you find that there are truly no happy times, you need to evaluate your situation. Are you the one who is perceiving everything as unhappy? If so, you might want to talk to a mental health professional. Depression can be treated. You have been through a lot and there is nothing wrong with finding someone who can help you deal with what you have experienced. If your child is the one who sees everything negatively, give the situation some thought. Is there something you are doing to add a negative edge to everything? Can you encourage your child to lighten up a bit? If nothing seems to help, your child might be suffering from depression as well. You need to find a mental health professional who is experienced in working with children and get some outside help. Be sure to discuss this with the other parent. You could also see a counselor with your child to help you sort out what is happening and how you can improve things. See Chapter 10 for information about what to do if the parenting schedule you have is simply not working and is causing problems for your child.

For the most part, you can expect there to be an end to unhappy times. You might find that there are some changes you can make to your life, to the visitation schedule, or to the way in which you deal with the other parent that can make huge improvements in the way you and your child view the world. It could be as simple as altering the time visitation starts or ends or agreeing not to discuss schedule changes in front of your child. Later chapters discuss these possibilities in greater detail.

Common symptoms of depression in adults, teens and children include:

➤ Persistent sad or irritable mood
➤ Loss of interest in activities once enjoyed
➤ Significant change in appetite or body weight
➤ Difficulty sleeping or oversleeping
➤ Psychomotor agitation or retardation
➤ Loss of energy
➤ Feelings of worthlessness or inappropriate guilt
➤ Difficulty concentrating
➤ Recurrent thoughts of death or suicide

Signs that may be associated with depression in children and teens:

➤ Frequent vague, non-specific physical complaints such as headaches, muscle aches, stomachaches or tiredness
➤ Frequent absences from school or poor performance in school
➤ Talk of or efforts to run away from home
➤ Outbursts of shouting, complaining, unexplained irritability, or crying
➤ Being bored
➤ Lack of interest in playing with friends
➤ Alcohol or substance abuse

➤ Social isolation, poor communication
➤ Fear of death
➤ Extreme sensitivity to rejection or failure
➤ Increased irritability, anger, or hostility
➤ Reckless behavior
➤ Difficulty with relationships

(from The National Institute of Mental Health, National Institute of Health Publication No. 00-4744)

If you or your child have four or more symptoms, it is a good idea to see a therapist, counselor or doctor.

Anger and Resentment

Both you and your child probably feel some sort of anger or resentment towards each other and towards the other parent. This is normal. All families experience this at times. When you first discover that your child is angry with you, it may come as a great shock to you, but it really is a normal part of the adjustment process.

The Introduction and Chapter 1 discuss how to deal with and get past your own feelings, so now let's talk about how to help your child cope with his or hers. Many children will be frightened by their own feelings and unable to understand or verbalize what they are really experiencing. You are not a therapist; you are a parent. No one expects you to be able to handle these feelings perfectly. Of course, it hurts you to think your child is angry. Of course, it just makes you even angrier at the other parent and at yourself. Of course, it makes you sick to think that your child may blame himself or herself for the divorce, separation or visitation scenario. You might also feel angry with your child about the way he or she is treating you. Your reaction is normal, and so is your child's.

The first thing you must do, even if you are a person who does not often talk about feelings, is to tell your child flat out that absolutely none of this is his or her fault and that nothing could have been done to change any of it. Children don't automatically know this. They need to be told. You will need to tell your child this on many occasions before it will really sink in. You need to tell your child that you love him or her very much and that nothing will ever change that. Reassure your child that you will always be a part of his or her life and that the other parent will as well. You should tell your child that it is perfectly fine for him or her to be angry at you, at the other parent and at the world if necessary. Say that you want your child to tell you about anything that bothers him or her. You need to really listen to what your child says. Try not to categorize or define the feelings for him or her and let them come out and accept them without judgment.

Next, you need to open up a little bit about yourself. Tell your child that you are sorry that there was a divorce or end of relationship and that it has been hard for you, too.

DO NOT SAY ANYTHING BAD
ABOUT THE OTHER PARENT.

You need to talk about your *feelings* only. Your child needs to know that you have experienced hurt, sadness and anger, but your child also needs to know that you are going to move forward and that you will always have lots of time and space in your life for the child. You should not dwell on what you are going through. You are talking to a child, not a friend or confidant.

Emphasize that what happened with the other parent had only to do with your marriage or relationship. Explain that he or she will always be the child's mom or dad and that you will always support that. It is also important to say that you are all still a family, but in a different way.

While all of the above might sound pretty simplistic and more appropriate for younger children, teens need to get this same message from you. Your teen may not be willing to discuss these things, but they are things that you need to say.

Do not expect this talk to be a cure-all. Instead, see it as a beginning. Keep the lines of communication open and try to find a way to talk about problems and feelings instead of yelling about them or closing up. It takes a lot of time to work through these things and there is no quick fix.

There may be a time when your child or teen says something like, "I hate you," or "I wish you weren't my mom/dad." These are difficult words to hear, but they are fairly common. Don't panic, flip out or blow your top. Hearing your child say something like this hurts you, but remember that your child does not truly mean it. In the heat of the moment, it sounds pretty believable, but you have to remember that your child is, in fact, just a child. Teens may seem fairly adult sometimes, but they too are prone to these comments.

You can't expect him or her to have a mature reaction or take the time to really process his or her feelings in a complicated way. The best way to handle this is to either not react at all or to calmly say, "I'm sorry you feel that way." Don't try to get into a lengthy discussion or try to convince your child he or she is wrong. This really will pass. It is a temporary and very common reaction.

Your child may also say something at some point indicating that he or she blames you entirely for the divorce or separation. This is also common. Pre-teens and teens sometimes reach a point where they decide they have the entire situation figured out and can assign blame to one parent. This is a tough period to work through. You have to remain calm, even though inside you are furious that your child thinks this (or in your opinion has been brainwashed to think this). You can tell your child that a divorce or separation is never one person's fault and that there are always lots of reasons for it that only the people who were in the situation could ever truly understand. Don't get into all the reasons why you believe the other parent is at fault.

Dealing with the Fear of Abandonment

Your child has lost his or her nuclear family. One or both parents have moved to new residences. You and the other parent have decided that you don't want to live together anymore. Your child may naturally fear that his or her parents may decide that they don't love him or her next. Even teens have this kind of subconscious fear. Everything in your child's universe has been substantially altered. Think for a moment how terrifying that is.

You need to let your child know that you are not abandoning him or her. Mom and Dad have decided to change some things about where and how they live and it has nothing to do with the child. He or she has a home at both places now, and there will *always* be a place for him or her.

Neither parent can ever decide not to love their child. Explain that there is a difference in the way moms and dads love each other and the way they love their kids. Moms and dads choose each other and decide to live together. They can decide not to live together. Parents and kids don't choose each other and can't decide they don't want to be together anymore.

Loving a spouse is like wearing a hat. You can take it off if you want to, if you have to, or if it gets uncomfortable. Loving a child is like having a head. You can never take it off, get rid of it, or truly change it. It is a part of you always. If your child is a teen, this explanation is too basic. You do need to state that people in a marriage can change how they feel, but that parents cannot change how they feel about their children. Remember that your child or teen does not know what it feels like to feel a parent's love for a child. Explain how it makes you feel and how it is a part of you that can never change.

You need to explain that you were not trying to keep the child away from the other parent when you asked for and got sole or residential custody. Explain that a child has to have one home and it seemed to you and to the judge (and to the other parent if he or she agreed with this) that the best place for this home was with you. He or she still has two parents and he or she will continue to have a home with both of you.

Some children feel a little lost when they begin to go with the other parent for visitation. Even teens have a hard time adjusting. Give your child a card with your phone numbers on it and tell him or her that it is OK to call you from the other parent's home anytime just to talk. Sometimes children need to be able to touch base with the parent they are not physically with. You should also tell your child that it is perfectly fine for him or her to call the other parent from your home at any time. You need to keep the lines of communication open in both directions. For older children and teens, use email as another communication option. Make sure your teen knows he or she can call or email anytime just to touch base.

You can help your child feel more comfortable with visitation by explaining in advance what will happen. Make sure he or she knows when it starts and when it ends. Be aware that as children grow older, they may have different reactions to visitation. Just because your child settles in and accepts visitation initially, does not mean that problems will not arise with it down the line.

Dealing with Divided Loyalties

Children of divorce often feel pulled in two directions. They want to take both parents' sides. When with Mom they will say bad things about Dad and vice versa. They want to please whomever they are with. Children feel confused and angry. The best way to cope with divided loyalties is to acknowledge they are going to happen and not encourage them. Never discuss your unpleasant feelings or opinions about the other parent with the child. Do not try to get your child to see your side of the story. Don't try to convince the child that you are in the right and the other parent is in the wrong.

There should not be any "sides" as far as your children are concerned. Your children have two parents who love them, but who disagree about some things. The disagreements are not something the children need to be involved in or concern themselves with. If your child expresses opinions about the other parent, be available to listen, but do not become involved with the conflict by intervening, agreeing with the child or criticizing the other parent. Talk to the other parent about this and see if you can both agree not to do these things. If the other parent does try to play on the divided loyalties, you should not do so in retaliation. Stand your ground. Read more about this in Chapter 6.

Dealing with Your Changing Feelings

You need to realize that you are going to experience changes in the way you feel as your new life as a custodial parent plays out. There are going to be days when your child is with the other parent and you know you will simply die if you can't see your child. You can get through these days by going on one moment at a time. Look forward to the next time you will be together or think about good times you have had in the past. Distract yourself with work, friends or family. Alcohol (or drugs) will not help you distract yourself and will only make the entire situation worse and endanger your relationship with your child. There will also be days where you are happy to find yourself with the freedom to go anywhere and do anything without parenting obligations. You are not a bad parent for enjoying some freedom.

You will find that your feelings towards your child may change. Some days you will feel like you know everything about your child, and other days he or she may be like a stranger who has a whole other life that you are excluded from. When you feel very connected and comfortable, let your child know. Give hugs, say how happy you are feeling or just enjoy it. If you feel excluded, ask questions and make conversation so you can feel included, but never, ever accuse your child of leaving you out or cutting you off. You want to convey positive or constructive feelings whenever possible. If your child really is trying to exclude you, calmly explain that you would like to be involved in his or her life or activities. Discuss it without placing blame on the child.

All of your feelings are real and important, but they are not all appropriate to share with your child. Confide in a friend or relative, but keep your child off your emotional roller coaster.

There will be times when you are angry with your child. This doesn't make you a bad parent. Before the marriage or relationship ended, there were times when you became angry with your child. It is normal to have this happen occasionally. Be certain that you control your anger, but feel free to be human and express it reasonably.

Dealing with Your Child's Changing Feelings

Just as you are on an emotional roller coaster, so is your child. One day she refuses to go on visitation and the next day she demands to go to the other parent's house. Your best bet is to not react in the heat of the moment. Count to ten if you have to before reacting. Be loving and supportive. This does not mean that anything your child does can be excused because of the trauma of divorce or separation. There are standards of behavior that your child must meet and as the parent, you are the one to set them and enforce them. You can give some leeway when needed, but you can't allow a child's emotions to control you or your life. Chapter 5 deals with this in-depth. Just keep in mind that all of these extreme moods cannot—and do not—last forever. Stick to your schedule and do not give in.

Many experts compare the divorce or separation adjustment process with the grieving process. Understand that your child has many stages and phases to go through in order to accept what has happened, just as you do. You also need to know that children often have delayed reactions to divorce or separation. They may not scream and shout when you tell them about the divorce or separation the first time. It may take months for their emotions to fully develop about the situation. As children grow older, they begin to process the divorce or separation differently and may have different reactions with each passing year. Be patient.

If you find that you need help dealing with your child's emotions, there are many things you can do. The first thing you should do is talk to the other parent, if possible. Compare notes and see if you can devise a solution together. Talk to a counselor or therapist. You can see a counselor and get some ideas for how to cope without having to involve your child in counseling, or you can have your child meet with a counselor if you like. Talk to your child's teacher. Teachers can often offer insights about a child's behavior.

Remember that children's emotions are not clear and they are not easily categorized. Talk about what is in front of you, but realize there may be more to it than you are hearing. Learn to ask non-critical, open-ended questions that will help draw your child out and bring a wide range of emotions to the forefront. Do not be afraid to get help from counselors or therapists.

Learn to roll with the punches when it comes to dealing with emotions. Learn to be responsive to them in an intelligent and thoughtful way. If your child is being clingy, you may want to change your plans to take him to a get- together with your friends. If she is determined to be angry with you, you might want to get out of the house and do something to take both of your minds off the situation or you might decide to just let him or her spend the afternoon listening to music. Be prepared to be flexible. Remember that you have feelings as well, and sometimes when they are going to clash with your child's feelings. You aren't going to handle all of this perfectly—no one expects you to. Be yourself and try to put parenting first on your list of priorities.

3

COMMUNICATING
WITH YOUR CHILD

Once you are living with a parenting schedule and not seeing your child every single day, it can become harder to feel as if you are communicating well with your child. While you are adjusting to the new schedule, you need to pay careful attention to how you are communicating with your child. Eventually things will become easier and you won't need to constantly monitor what you say or how you say it.

You are going through a difficult time and it is hard to control your emotions in a time with so much turmoil, but this is something you have to do for the sake of your child. It may seem too much to expect that you have to put your child first when you probably feel like nobody has put you first in a long time. But I promise you, it will be worth it. If you can take a few months and pay attention to your communications with your child, you will find that you will rebuild any bonds you might have thought were lost or damaged. There will also be times in the years ahead when it seems like communication with your child breaks down. Come back to this chapter and review the suggestions in it again then. You and your child have a long road ahead that you need to walk together. Building your communication and trust today can only help you in the years ahead.

What You *Should* Say to Your Child

After a divorce or a separation, you need to verbalize things that you wouldn't normally feel a need to verbalize. You probably would not normally feel a need to tell your child, "I could never hate you," or, "You will always be an important part of my life." These seem obvious to you, but you need to reassure your child about your love and commitment to him or her. You also need to offer your child a reasonable amount of praise. You will want to have a conversation with your child about the divorce or separation in which you can act as if you are not angry and filled with hate for the other spouse (even if you are!). You need to let your child know you support his or her relationship with the other parent. At the same time, you do not want to be over the top, insincere, or do something that is not part of your personality. Be yourself, but try to focus on verbalizing these things to your child in some way. It is also not something you should harp on. Talk about it when you need to.

It is often hard to know how much to say when answering children's questions about divorce or separation. The best approach is to be honest, yet not harsh, negative, or too detailed. Give a general answer to the question without blaming the other parent.

It's important to talk to your child about things that are happening in the present—what you are doing together, what he or she is thinking or feeling now. Get involved in the present and let the past go. You can't change what has happened, but you can dramatically affect how you relate to each other now and how involved you are in each other's lives from here on out. It is also important to plan together for the future.

Be positive when you talk about the other parent. Emphasize his or her strengths and good points. Your child will often tell you things that happen at the other home. It is fine to listen and ask a few informational questions but you should NOT use your child as a spy to learn what the other parent is doing or what goes on in the other home. For example, encourage your child to ask Mom for help with math homework, since Mom is good at math, or comment that it was nice of Dad to take him or her ice-skating.

Things You *Should Not* Say

You should *never* say anything negative about the other parent. Think how hurt you would be if someone told you that one of your parents was a liar, unfaithful, cruel or selfish. It is OK to let your child know that you and the other parent have differences, but it is not OK to insult, degrade, or detail what is wrong with the other parent.

You should *never* suggest that your child has to pick between the two of you or suggest that he or she favors one parent over the other. It is very common for children to try to please the parent they are with by declaring that they love that parent more and then turn around and say the exact same to the other parent when with him or her. Don't get involved in these love contests.

You do not need to share the details of your emotional situation with your child. It is fine to say that you feel sad about the divorce, but you should *never* discuss details about your anger, hurt, depression or betrayal with your child. He or she is not a friend for you to lean on. It is alright to let a child know you are seeing a therapist to help you work some problems out or that you are taking medication for a depressive illness. These are not things you should hide or be embarrassed about.

Financial issues are not something that should be discussed with children. While it is acceptable to say that you cannot afford to buy the leather jacket/tv/video game/movie/toy your child is asking for, you should not go into details about the financial aspects of the divorce or support payments.

Your child is not a messenger or a spy. Do not send messages to the other parent through your child or pump your child for information about the other parent. Not only does this place your child in a terrible position (one where no one is pleased and the child feels that he or she has betrayed you both), but the information you get or that the child conveys is not accurate most of the time. The stress a child feels in a situation like this is incredible.

You cannot rely on a child to give you insights into the other parent's life, nor can you rely on a child to convey difficult messages accurately. If your child tells you, "There was a strange lady at Daddy's house," it could mean anything from a drop off by UPS to a meeting with his insurance agent. Don't try to read into what your child tells you.

You also cannot ask your child to keep secrets from the other parent. If there is something you don't want the other parent to find out about, don't let your child know. Otherwise, anticipate that the child will talk to the other parent.

Don't make promises you can't keep. Your child will be disappointed and will learn not to trust you. It is OK to be optimistic, though. Say, "It would be fun to go to Disneyworld sometime," instead of, "I'll take you to Disneyworld next year."

Listening to Your Child

To truly communicate with your child, you need to listen to what he or she is telling you, verbally and non-verbally. Pay attention to his or her reactions to things and draw conclusions.

Ask open-ended questions of your child to get him or her to open up. Show interest in the things he or she is doing and thinking about. Listen to what he or she is talking about and respond.

Expect children under age 8 to ask repeated questions about the divorce or separation, the schedule, the other parent, etc. Answer these questions even if you feel as if you already did. The repetition will show the child that this new world he or she is living in is dependable. Your child may, at some point, say he or she would rather live with the other parent. Usually this happens when the two of you are having some problems, but it is also common from an older child who is the same sex as the other parent. Find out why your child is asking before becoming defensive. There are times when a change of custody is appropriate, but often this is your child's way of pointing out a problem or bonding with the other parent.

THINGS TO SAY TO YOUR CHILD

- ➤ I love you.
- ➤ You are always going to be part of my family.
- ➤ I am happy to be with you.
- ➤ I am so proud of the way you ____. (fill in the blank)
- ➤ I know this is difficult for you.
- ➤ I am always willing to listen to anything you need to talk about.
- ➤ This is your home, and Mom's/Dad's house is your home as well.
- ➤ Your mother/father and I disagree about some things and that's OK.
- ➤ Mom/Dad and I divorced each other, but not you. We will always be your parents and we will work hard to be parents together.
- ➤ One of the reasons we got divorced was because we disagreed about too many things, but you and I can disagree and you don't have to worry that we will ever lose each other.
- ➤ Moms and dads can get divorced but parents and kids never can.
- ➤ Your mom/dad will always be your mom/dad. That's how I want it.
- ➤ This is the schedule we are going to be using. I'd like to know how you feel about it.
- ➤ When we are not together, I think about you and am happy to know I will be seeing you again soon.
- ➤ You can call Mom/Dad anytime you want to.
- ➤ How did _____ (fill in the blank) go at school today?
- ➤ What did you do at your friend Dylan's house yesterday?
- ➤ What would you like to do tonight?
- ➤ We are using this schedule because we think it is the best way to share our time with you. We both would be with you all the time if we could, but we can't.
- ➤ We are not going to get back together. I know that would make you happy, but the divorce is final and we won't change our minds.
- ➤ Why don't you ask Mom/Dad to help you with that. He/She is good at things like that.
- ➤ Mom/Dad loves you and always has.
- ➤ Mom/Dad and I got divorced because we disagreed a lot and fought too much.
- ➤ It isn't anyone's fault that we got divorced. Sometimes marriages just don't work out.
- ➤ How great that Mom/Dad took you to the zoo. What did you see there?
- ➤ I think that if you are upset about what happened at Mom's/Dad's house, you should talk to her/him about it.

Things *Not* to Say to Your Child

➤ Your mother/father is dishonest/mean/stupid/cruel/lazy/cheap, etc.

➤ You are going to have to choose which parent you want to be with.

➤ Wouldn't you rather be with me this weekend? We could do anything you wanted.

➤ You always side with your mother/father.

➤ You are just like your mother/father.

➤ Ever since the divorce I have felt so alone.

➤ Don't tell Mom/Dad we did this.

➤ Which one of us do you love more?

➤ I want you to know that this is all your mother's/father's fault.

➤ When you leave, I am all alone.

➤ Don't you wish you could see me more?

➤ It's OK if you don't want to go to Mom's/Dad's.

➤ Sometimes I just want to kill myself.

➤ We can't go to the movies because your mother/father took all the money from me in the divorce.

➤ Who was that man/woman at the house when I picked you up?

➤ Where is Mom/Dad going tonight?

➤ I don't get enough child support to buy you a new coat.

➤ I have to get a job because Mom/Dad doesn't give us enough money to live on.

➤ Tell Mom/Dad you need to be home by 7 instead of 8.

➤ If your mother/father didn't waste all his/her money on shoes/beer, I might get enough child support to buy you the new __ you want.

➤ Tell your mother/father I need that check by Friday or I'm taking him/her to court.

➤ You always have an attitude when you come back from there.

➤ You should tell Mon/Dad that you love me more.

➤ It is disgusting that he/she bought a new car and I don't have enough to pay for your school lunches.

➤ Watch out for men/women. They take what they want and throw you aside.

➤ Don't ever get married. You'll regret it.

➤ You can just tell him/her that if you aren't home on time next week, I'm calling the police.

4

RULES FOR YOUR CHILD

The most important thing for a child who has experienced a divorce or separation is normalcy. Children need to feel that, although their parents' relationship has drastically changed, many things in their own lives will remain stable. It is crucial that now, more than ever, your child feels that there are things in life that he or she can count on.

One of the best ways to help a child feel rooted, protected and loved, is to have rules. Think about what life was like when you and the other parent lived together. You had a set of rules your child was expected to follow. In most families, these rules are unspoken, but everyone understands what they are. Children usually have some chores they are responsible for; there are set times for things such as meals, baths and homework, and there is behavior and speech that is not acceptable.

Now that you and the other parent have divorced or separated, it is important that your child continue to have rules and responsibilities. Life goes on and maintaining rules and continuing to expect certain things will demonstrate this to your child.

Some parents feel as if they should give their child a break. After all, he or she has been through a lot and expecting him or her to take out the garbage or clean the rabbit cage seems like an extra burden. Continuing to live normal lives where everyone has responsibilities and jobs is the best way to help your child get on track with the new situation. Life isn't carefree and easy and it is silly to pretend that it can be. Of course it is fine to make exceptions to the rules, but you've got to have the rules or your everyday life will just fall apart.

NOTE TO PARENTS WITH SOLE CUSTODY

You will notice that in this section and in other parts of the book, it is recommended that you and the other parent try to work together as parents—making rules and decisions about your child together. If you have legal sole custody (see Chapter _ for an explanation of the different types of custody), you are not legally obligated to do this. However, you should know that this is the best way to help your child through the situation. If you were given sole decision-making power by the court, there is probably a good reason for that. If you feel that you do not wish to include the other parent in the decision-making process, that is your right and you may be completely justified in this regard. You need to assess your situation and determine if it is possible to include the other parent in these decisions at all. If it is not, then you should focus on encouraging and developing your child's relationship with the other parent, while making sure that you handle the major decisions such as medical care, religion, schooling, and other activities. You need to remember that you cannot control what happens at the other parent's home and the best way to impact what happens there is to talk about it calmly and rationally with the other parent. The other parent is free to create rules at his or her own home (within reason and that do not cause harm to the child) and you cannot demand to be part of that decision-making process. For example, if your four-year-old has a bedtime of 8 P.M. at your home, but the other parent allows her to stay up until 9:30 P.M., you aren't going to be able to make the other parent to change this. You can, however, point out that your child is tired and cranky the next day, and suggest the other parent talk with the preschool teacher to learn how it is impacting the child at school.

Whose Rules: Yours or the Other Parent's

In an ideal world, the rules that were in place before the divorce or separation are the rules that you should continue to use. This will give your child a sense of continuity and will also lessen the potential for disagreement with your child and with the other parent.

In reality, most parents find that they do need to make changes to house rules after a divorce. Schedules change, as do the children's emotional needs, and nothing can ever be as it was. You may feel since you are now the only parent in your household that you should be able to set the rules in your household. If you feel this way, you are right to a certain extent. It is your home and you can decide how you will live and what rules you will follow. Taking responsibility for your own rules is an important part of coping with divorce. However, it is important to remember that your child now has two homes to live in and two parents to obey separately. It is just simpler if the rules in both homes are the same or very similar, particularly if your child is very young. Coordinating in this way lets your child know that you and the other parent will continue to parent together and that there is still a family unit that has importance in the child's life.

Creating Rules Together

Arrange to speak to the other parent (when your child is not around) and say you would like to discuss the rules that your child will be following in both homes. Explain that you believe it makes sense for both of you to have rules for your child that are the same or similar and you would like to work together to create rules that will work in both homes. You could show the other parent the information about this in the other half of this book to help explain the importance.

RULES TO DISCUSS WITH THE OTHER PARENT

➤ bedtime;

➤ wake-up time;

➤ how often bathing should occur;

➤ when homework should be done;

➤ household chores (there will be differences between the households, but the main point is that there should be some at each home and the time and difficulty level should be similar);

➤ unacceptable behavior, language and attitudes from you child;

➤ unacceptable foods or limits on certain foods for your child (for example, some doctors recommend limiting daily juice intake in babies, toddlers and preschoolers. There are similar recommendations for soda intake for older children and teens. Some children have food allergies, while others have religious restrictions on diet.);

➤ school attendance;

➤ when medication must be taken;

➤ the standard by which the child must keep his or her room clean;

➤ church and religious class attendance;

➤ when friends may come over and when the child may visit friends;

➤ curfew;

➤ amount of television time;

➤ amount of telephone time;

➤ amount of computer/video game time;

➤ teeth brushing, flossing and other hygiene;

➤ naps (for younger children); and,

➤ anything else either of you feel is important.

The goal is to try to keep most of the rules the same at both homes, but you and the other parent will probably find that some rules need adjustments. It is also important to remember that you may not agree about all of the rules. In that case, you will need to compromise—you could decide one rule and the other parent could decide another, or else you could reach a decision on a rule that is halfway between your two opinions (an 8:30 bedtime if one person says 8 and one says 9). You may also realize that some rules need to be different in each home. If this is what you both agree will work best, then it's fine. If you absolutely cannot reach an agreement or compromise, then you will each have to set your own rules.

You will gradually reach a point where you don't need to discuss certain rules. You aren't going to be spending the rest of your lives negotiating rules with the other parent. Eventually things will evolve to a point where most things are understood and don't require long discussions. As your child grows up and reaches new milestones (starting school, getting braces, getting his or her driver's license, getting a job, beginning to date, joining a sports team, and so on), it will be helpful to talk with the other parent about rules again, so you can coordinate with each other about rules for the changing situation.

Discussing Rules with Your Child

If most of the rules will remain the same as before the divorce or separation, it probably won't be necessary for you to have a formal conversation with your child about them. Just make them a part of your daily life when the child is at your home. If something will be changing, discuss it with your child. It is likely there will be different rules for some things at each home. Help your child understand and adjust to this. Some parents find that it is useful to post the house rules at each home, especially if you have a child that has trouble handling rules.

SAMPLE HOUSE RULES LIST

The rules of this house are as follows:
1. We do not yell at each other or hit each other.
2. We always treat each other with respect and kindness.
3. Bedtime is at 9:00 P.M. on school nights and 9:30 P.M. on other nights.
4. Dirty laundry is to be placed in the hamper.
5. Everyone must clear his or her own dishes off the table.
6. Jahleesa is responsible for folding all of the laundry.
7. Every Tuesday night the hamster cage will be cleaned out by Jamal.
8. Homework must be done before TV or computer time.
9. If you spill it, you clean it up.
10. All beds must be made before breakfast.
11. We will take turns loading the dishwasher.
12. Whoever is home on Saturday morning will help clean the house.
13. Phone calls are limited to no more than 20 minutes.

Some younger children benefit from a sticker chart, where the child gets a sticker placed on the chart for each chore that is done or every rule that is followed that day. If the child receives a sticked in each category for a day or a week, a special reward, like a video or a small toy, can help reinforce the behavior.

SAMPLE STICKER CHART

Cara's Sticker Chart	Mon.	Tues.	Wed.	Thurs.	Fri.	Sat.	Sun.
Put away her toys							
Did not throw anything							
Brushed her teeth							
Played nicely with dog							
Carried her dishes to the sink							
Washed her hands before eating							
Placed her shoes beside her bed							
Was quiet while adults were talking							

Some parents of teens find they like to have a contract with their child. A contract makes the teen take an active role in acknowledging and agreeing to the rules.

SAMPLE CONTRACT WITH TEEN

Chase White and his father Tom White enter into this contract and agree to follow it for the next 4 months.

1. The parties agree that they will not swear or shout.
2. On the days Chase is home, he will take out the trash, make his bed, and help do the dishes.
3. Chase will do his homework before he goes out with friends or watches TV.
4. Chase will set his alarm and make sure he is on time for school.
5. Chase will be home by 11 P.M. on weekends when he is home. If he is late, he will be grounded the next weekend day he is here.
6. Chase will not ride in a car with an unlicensed driver.
7. Chase will not have female guests over when Tom is not home.
8. Chase will earn $20 for every grade higher than a B on his report card.
9. Tom will not work on Sundays when Chase is home and will spend the day with him instead.

_____   _____   _____   _____
Chase Williams   date   Thomas Williams   date

The contract contains all of the rules and consequences the teen must follow. Both parents and the child sign it and agree to follow it. Sometimes these contracts also list what responsibilities the parents are committing to (listening to the child non-judgmentally, attending the child's sporting or extra-curricula events, and providing transportation to outings with friends, etc.).

Creating Your Own Rules

Because you now live on your own and your lifestyle has changed, there will be situations that arise at your home that were never an issue when you lived as a family. For example, your child may now arrive after school to an empty house. You will need rules to deal with situations like these. You don't need to initiate a discussion about these decisions with the other parent, since they happen at your house—unless you would like to get some input. Realize though that the other parent may hear about these new things and wish to discuss them with you. Don't view this as an attempt by the other parent to question your authority or undermine you. Briefly and calmly give a simple explanation. The other parent's involvement in your child's life is a good thing.

The Other Parent's Rules

The flip side to this is that things have changed for the other parent as well. He or she may find it necessary to formulate some new rules that pertain to new situations that are happening at that home. You may hear about things that concern you from your child. Calmly ask the other parent about these new situations and rules so that you can be informed. Remember that you have no authority to dictate what the rules will be in the other home, but you do have the right to understand them so you can know what your child is doing, and so that you can support the rules. It is also important that you do not question the basis for these rules in front of your child.

As a parent, your job is to help your child obey and live with rules, no matter who has created them and whether they are right or wrong. You would not suggest to your child that his or her teacher is wrong and that a rule at school should not be obeyed because you don't agree with it. You need to respect the other parent's rules in the same way.

Rules That Are Wrong

You and the other parent clearly have different opinions about some things—that's why you are no longer together. Occasions will arise where you feel the other parent has made a rule that is wrong. The best way to handle this is to discuss it with him or her when your child is not present. You also have to learn to step back and evaluate just how important this is.

If the other parent has a rule that your child must vacuum his or her room when he or she arrives at the other home, and you feel that it is excessive, take a look at the situation. Is this rule going to do serious harm to your child? Just because a child is unhappy about a rule does not mean it is wrong. If the other parent has a rule that the child may cross a busy street alone, and you believe the child is too young and could be harmed, then you do need to make an effort to get the other parent to change the rule by having a calm and reasonable discussion about it. See Chapter 6 for more information about communicating with the other parent. If you feel rules persist at the other home that are dangerous to your child or are completely unreasonable, you need to speak to your attorney or get outside help as discussed in Chapter 12. The same thing applies to discipline that you feel is dangerous or completely unreasonable.

Misinformation

When dealing with the other parent's rules, you have to remember that what your child tells you may not be entirely correct or complete. Kids can twist things a bit, sometimes because their perceptions or memories are wrong and sometimes to get a reaction out of you. Before you fly off the handle, get the information from the other parent. Things usually aren't as bad as they sound and even if something seems wrong on its face, an explanation from the other parent may show why it was necessary. You may also find your child did not give you all the details and left some important things out.

Bending the Rules

When you lived together as a family, there were times when the rules were bent or even completely thrown out the window on occasion. A special family gathering may have resulted in a late bedtime, a busy week may have meant household chores were skipped, and so on. Just because you are trying to provide continuity and stability does not mean you are a prison guard. It is perfectly fine to bend the rules and make exceptions, as long as you don't do it all the time. Flexibility is an important part of parenting.

Changing Rules for Your Changing Child

If your child is 8 years old and has an 8:30 P.M. bedtime, soon he or she will be older and able to stay up later. As children get older, many things in their lives change—amount of homework, curfew, eating habits, sleep needs, time with friends, etc. Rules for some of these things just gradually change with the child. Other times, you need to formally change a rule. When you notice that a rule needs to be changed, try to discuss it with the other parent. Probably he or she has noticed the same thing and probably both of you have begun to make adjustments.

As your child gets older, and as the trauma of the divorce or separation gets farther into the past, your child will be more comfortable with the notion of two homes and having some rules that are different at each home will no longer be as difficult to handle. You will eventually reach a point where things are run one way at your home and another way at the other parent's home and it is no longer a problem for anyone.

When Rules Are Broken

Part of having rules is having consequences when they are broken. When you and the other parent meet to discuss what the basic rules will be, you need to discuss what the appropriate types of repercussions are for broken rules. Some parents find it helpful to write these down. You need to agree that you won't question the other parent's use of these consequences and will not interfere with them.

It is important to discuss whether punishments will apply at both homes. For example, if your teen breaks curfew at your home and is grounded by you for three days, will this be three consecutive days and apply at whichever home the child is at or will it only apply to the next three days the child is at your home? You need to decide together how to handle these situations.

It is also important to note that mental health experts generally discourage the use of physical punishment. Physical punishment is never a good idea and can be especially dangerous when you have a former spouse on the look out for child abuse. Protect yourself and your child and avoid physical punishment.

Final Thoughts About Rules

When you and your child are first adjusting to life after divorce or separation, there will be conflict about rules and the child will find many opportunities to tell you that you are being unfair or that your rules are not the same as the other parent's. Also, as your child grows older, he or she may complain that some rules are now unfair. This is normal. It is part of adjusting and part of growing up. Your job is to hold steady and don't give in (other than once in a while), unless you truly believe a rule needs to be changed. Make sure you take the time to talk to your child about rules and listen to and consider his or her input. Eventually, you will find that you get into a routine where every little rule is no longer questioned. Don't give up just because things get rocky. Your child will love and respect you more if you have consistent and fair rules that are evenly applied, even if he or she squawks in the short term.

Keep in mind that in order for your child to grow up believing that he or she is still part of a family, and that he or she has two parents who love and believe in him or her, you need to demonstrate respect and consideration for the other parent. Even if you believe he or she has random rules and ineffective punishments, don't tell your child. Be a model for your child by showing him or her that it is important to treat other people with respect and consideration (despite their behaviors), and that rules must be followed no matter how random or wrong they are. Encourage your child to voice his or her opinion about rules, but remind him or her that parents make the rules. You and the other parent are still parenting together and in order to do so, you must support each other's decisions, rules and consequences.

5

RULES FOR YOURSELF

In order for your custody and visitation plan to work, you need to con-sciously make an effort to make it work. Just because you are now divorced and living by yourself as a single parent does not mean that things are going to be free and easy for you. Things are going to be dif-ficult for a while until you, your child, and the other parent have adjusted to your new lives. To get through the difficult adjustment period and create a plan for the future, you need to have some rules for yourself. There will also be times in the future when things will become difficult. Return to this chapter then to help yourself cope.

Dealing with Your Emotions

You have a lot to cope with in terms of your feelings of loss, anger, frus-tration, depression, love, grief and fear. Allow yourself to recognize what you are feeling and deal with it. Suppressing and denying your feelings is not the answer. However, you do have to find a way to con-trol your emotions around your child and the other parent. You and your child need to focus on maintaining your relationship, not on rehashing the divorce. Your feelings about the divorce or separation are for *you* to deal with. Your child has an enormous amount of emotions to handle without trying to cope with or understand yours. Resolve to control your emotions as best as you can.

You and the other parent are no longer emotional partners and you need to separate yourself from him or her emotionally, while continu-ing to parent together. Resolve to try to work together.

Thinking About the Other Parent

Some custodial parents believe that because the court gave them sole or residential custody of their child that they have been appointed Head Parent. This is not the case. Parenting must always be a joint effort. Certainly each parent will be in charge of the child at different times, but at no time is either parent in charge of the other. Thinking that you can direct the other parent to do things, change his or her behavior, or tell him or her what he or she can or cannot do with the child will only lead to trouble. Try to adopt a cooperative approach to the other parent. Don't think of him or her not as the enemy, a less capable parent, or someone who needs your guidance. Remember that you are not in charge of his or her parenting. It is best if you can find a way to communicate with each other, and share concerns and opinions about your child. This has to be done in a way that allows you to respect each other's parenting rights and give each other space too. You cannot act like the victor, the righteous and the anointed best parent, even if you secretly believe this to be the case.

If you want to have input into the way the other parent does things, you'll catch more flies with honey than vinegar. Offer suggestions, helpful hints, and information, but avoid sounding as if you are issuing commands, making demands or laying down the law. Resolve to try to be polite and to keep negative thoughts to yourself.

Talking About the Other Parent

Your child does still have another parent and spends time with that parent. You can't pretend that the other parent doesn't exist. Your child will talk about the other parent because he or she is an important part of the child's life. You should not stop your child from discussing the other parent.

You do need to monitor what comes out of your own mouth about the other parent. Resolve to never say anything derogatory, insulting, cruel, or negative about the other parent. That doesn't mean you can't think it—just don't say it. Your child loves the other parent and will always have a relationship with him or her. You must allow this and you must not try to get your child to see the other parent's "true colors." You need to be encouraging about the time the child spends with the other parent. Let him or her have a separate relationship with the other parent and allow him or her to draw his or her own conclusions.

Just as you must bite your tongue sometimes when speaking to the other parent (see Chapter 6 for guidelines about this), there are times when you need to bite your tongue around your child. Don't let negative comments about the other parent slip out. Never negatively compare your child to the other parent. ("You're thoughtless just like your mother.") Don't talk all about you—what you are doing, what you are feeling, etc. Of course, you must share some of your thoughts and feelings in order to have a good relationship with your child, but it shouldn't be all about you.

Avoid talking about everything that went wrong in the relationship with the other parent and your longing for the past. That being said, you cannot act as though the past never happened. It is normal and healthy to mention something that sparks a memory you share. ("That's just like the time we went camping and Dad got lost in the woods.")

Try to avoid being overly critical of your child while you are all adjusting to your new lives or to a recent change in the situation. You are bound to be more irritable, more easily hurt, and more easily annoyed during this period. You have to find a way to monitor what comes out of your mouth.

There will probably be a time when your child complains to you about the other parent. Resolve to listen to what the child has to say but do not become involved in the dispute. A good answer is to tell the child that you are glad he or she feels comfortable telling you about this, but that it is something he or she needs to discuss with the other parent. The exception to this is if your child is in danger or is extremely upset. See Chapter 8 for information about how to intervene.

Respecting Visitation
Respecting your child's time with and feelings for the other parent is an important rule to make for yourself. Support and encourage their relationship. This doesn't mean you have to be a cheerleader, but it does mean you should not discourage visitation or say negative things about the other parent.

Avoiding Confrontations
Avoid arguments and non-productive discussions with the other parent, especially in front of your child. Try to be as civil as possible to the other parent. It won't always be easy, but it will help your child. See Chapter 6 for more about this.

Talking About the Divorce or Separation
There will be times when your child will ask you questions about why you divorced and how you feel about the other parent. It is important

to be honest, yet not negative. Instead of saying, "Your mother is selfish and I couldn't put up with it anymore," or, "Your father was sleeping around," you should give an answer like, "Mom and I disagreed about a lot of things," or, "Dad and I decided that we wanted to live our lives differently." It's important to make it clear that neither parent is at fault and that you will not be getting back together. Resolve to answer questions honestly, but without unnecessary or hurtful details.

Promises to Your Child

Don't make promises you can't keep. Period.

It is much better to be honest with your child. If your child does not want to go on visitation, instead of promising that he or she will not have to, explain why it is important for him or her to go. Say you miss him or her too, and that you are sad when you are apart, but that you focus on how happy it will be the next time you are together and how much fun he or she will have with the other parent. Make promises that are realistic. If you have to break a promise, be honest about it and tell your child right away. Explain what has happened and why you can't keep your promise.

Being on Time

It is important that you set up parenting transfer times for times when you are available. Waiting at the window for your car to arrive for 45 minutes or sitting in the driveway with the other parent waiting for you to get home will upset your child and send a message that you do not care. Your child already has some feelings of abandonment. Don't make them worse. When you have made a commitment to being with your child, be on time. It is also important to be on time if you are dropping the child off at the other parent's home. Doing so will show the child and the other parent that you respect their relationship and support their time together.

Promise yourself that you will be on time. If you are going to be late for an unforeseen reason, call and let your child and the other parent know. If you find that you are regularly late, you need to make some schedule changes.

Making the Best of It

Being a divorced or separated parent is nobody's dream—the dream is a happy and cozy little family where nobody has to divide time. But the fact of the matter is that this is what you are, and you must find a way to live with it and make it work for you. You must promise yourself from the outset that you will make the most of the time you have with your child. This is different from setting unreasonably high expectations for yourself. It's not going to be perfect and it's not going to come easily. Give your child your full attention whenever possible, be emotionally available for your child and always look for the bright side. This doesn't mean you shouldn't have a life. You have a job, friends and family and you need to continue to live your life. You should not hole up in the house with your child. When you are active, happy, and fulfilled, you are a better parent. You do need to think about your child's emotions and remember to include your child in the new life you are building for yourself.

FOLLOW THESE RULES FOR YOURSELF

➤ Do not confide in your child about all of your feelings about the divorce or separation.

➤ Make real time for your child in your life.

➤ Respect your child's time with and feelings about the other parent.

➤ Be on time in all your dealings with your child.

➤ See yourself as emotionally separate from the other parent.

➤ Be honest about the fact that reconciliation is not going to happen.

➤ Find a way to cope with your emotions. See a therapist or talk with friends.

➤ Live your own life. To be a good parent, you must have your own life.

➤ Never speak negatively about the other parent in front of your child.

➤ Do not have expectations that are too high.

➤ Show your love for your child.

➤ Resolve to cope with your emotions and move on with your life.

➤ Maintain your job, your friendships and your family relationships.

➤ Find pleasure in life and pass this on to your child.

➤ Don't make promises to your child that you can't keep.

➤ Avoid confrontations with the other parent (see Chapter 6 for more information about communicating with the other parent).

➤ Expect things to be difficult for a while.

➤ Stop blaming yourself and focus on the positive things in your life.

➤ Make your home a place where you are comfortable.

➤ Plan to be civil to the other parent and to work with him or her to help your child have a better life.

6

COMMUNICATING WITH THE OTHER PARENT

It is likely that one of the reasons you and the other parent are no longer together is because you have difficulty communicating. You probably both harbor some negative feelings towards each other. Despite all of this, you are going to have to develop some way to talk to each other so that your child can receive the benefits of visitation. Even if you have a detailed, court-ordered visitation plan, problems and conflicts are going to arise that will require communication. Finding a way a to communicate will certainly not be easy, but it will make visitation easier, and will reduce stress for everyone involved.

Try to Develop a New Relationship

You and the other parent are going to be parents together for the rest of your lives. Even though you are divorced or not together anymore, the parenting part of your relationship continues. You will be parents together for the rest of your lives. It is a fact you cannot change and a bond you cannot break. Try to sit down and talk to each other simply as parents, not as two people whose marriage or relationship went bad. If you can both agree that you each want what is best for your child, then you can find a way to achieve it together. Resolve to be co-parents. Agree not to argue about past events and to talk only about the foreseeable future. It takes a lot of work and a lot of effort to develop a new parenting relationship with each other.

It is easy to fall back into your old patterns of arguing, disagreeing and trying to hurt each other. Agree that you will not let this happen. Think about how important your child is to you. You cannot change who your child's other parent is, no matter how much you might wish to. You also cannot change how the other parent behaves. You can only focus on finding a way to cooperate with him or her to make life better for your child.

You are both human and will both slip up. Accept that you will both break the rules once in a while, but try to get past the mistakes and focus on keeping your child's welfare as your priority. Remind yourself constantly that you are doing this for your child.

Set Visitation Rules for Yourselves

If you and the other parent are going to make visitation go smoothly, you need to set up some basic rules you will both follow. Here are some examples of rules that will help both of you cope:

> ➤ Schedule changes must be requested as soon as possible and preferably no later than 24 hours in advance.
> ➤ If the parent picking up or dropping off the child is going to be more than 15 minutes late, he or she will call.
> ➤ You each will try your best to accommodate schedule changes requested by the other parent.
> ➤ You will work together to create rules for your child.
> ➤ Decide who will be responsible for washing the clothes taken on visitation. You may be surprised to learn that this is often one of the most common problems that arises in dealing with visitation!
> ➤ Any items taken on visitation will be returned with the child (especially those crucial items—blankie, jacket, school books, instrument, sports uniforms, sneakers, favorite toy).
> ➤ Agree not to argue in front of your child. Whenever an argument starts, develop a word or phrase you will both recognize that will indicate this is something you should discuss later, out of earshot of your child (such as "later," "table it," etc.).
> ➤ Your child is not permitted to make changes in the visitation schedule without permission from both of you.
> ➤ You will not use your child to transmit messages or money to each other.
> ➤ You will contact each other directly, either in person, by phone or in writing.
> ➤ You will always check with each other if your child has a complaint about the other parent. Children's perceptions are often skewed and stories tend to grow as they are repeated to other people. Sometimes this is intentional and other times it is not. Always consult the other parent if the child is complaining about something serious before flying off the handle.

➤ The parent that the child is with at the time is responsible for transporting him or her to scheduled activities such as sports and classes.

➤ Decide who will be responsible for your child's meal if transfer time is scheduled near a normal meal time.

Think about what other ground rules you will need to have in place to facilitate visitation and add any that are helpful to your specific situation.

You probably know what your and the other parent's "hot spots" are. Try to avoid setting each other off and make some rules to help you do this.

Be Flexible

Flexibility is a must in making visitation work. Think of visitation as a give and take situation, not as giving in, letting the other parent win, or being victorious. If you let the other parent change weekends with you this time, then when you ask for a change, it shouldn't be a problem. This might mean you and the other parent will have to acknowledge and accept that you both have separate lives now and that won't be easy. This does not mean you should make changes on a regular basis. Your child needs stability. But some changes are OK. Do not feel that just because the judge told you to begin visitation at 5:30 P.M. on Wednesdays, that this is written in stone. You and the other parent can make any adjustments to the schedule as long as you both agree to do so. If 6:00 P.M. works better for both of you, then make that your scheduled time. Be prepared to have to make adjustments as your life, the other parent's life and your child's life change and grow. Visitation plans need to develop as situations do.

Develop a Written Schedule Together

Even if you have a court-ordered schedule, you should still calendar it out so that you both have a written schedule of where your child will be when. Plan out the schedule for the whole year, but do it in pencil. Then look at it and talk about what needs to be changed. If you have to go out of town when your child is supposed to be with you or if the other parent wants a weekend alone to prepare for an exam, make adjustments. Look at how the holidays will be divided and talk about whether or not they will work the way they are currently scheduled and make adjustments as needed. Plan out any vacations either of you will be taking with the child at this time as well. Remember to be flexible, reasonable and calm. Treat this the same way you would treat any other scheduling situation in your every-day life.

Bite Your Tongue

The most important thing to remember when dealing with the other parent is to think before you speak! Try not to have knee jerk responses to the things about him or her that irritate you. Try not to get angry or upset in front of the other parent. Go home and punch your pillow or scream in the shower afterwards, but do not get into confrontations. This does not mean you have to be a victim or give in on every point. Choose your battles carefully and try to minimize them. Be polite and courteous to the other parent even if you do not get the same treatment in return. Keep in mind that you are putting up with it all for the benefit of your child.

Divide Responsibilities

If the other parent was always the one to take your child for haircuts, maybe you wish to continue things this way. Perhaps you were the parent who handled all doctor appointments. It is a good idea to talk about these kinds of responsibilities and develop a plan for who will handle them. If not, you may make an appointment for your child's dental check up only to find the other parent made one as well. Decide who is going to be primarily in charge of:

- ➤ hair cuts
- ➤ medical, dental, vision and orthodontia check ups (sick visits will be handled by whomever is with the child when he or she becomes ill or injured)
- ➤ purchasing seasonal or once a year items like new shoes, boots, coats, school supplies, sports equipment and so on

Many parents agree to let the custodial parent handle these things, but involving the other parent will allow your child to feel as if both parents are involved in his or her life.

Arguments

Never, ever argue in front of your child if you can help it. Your child is already struggling to believe that the divorce or breakup is not his or her fault. When parents argue about visitation, all the child thinks is that "they are arguing because of me." Handle all disagreements when your child is not around.

Setting Up Times to Talk

Some parents find that they are best able to communicate with each other if they schedule a weekly or monthly meeting or phone call to discuss their child. Do so when you can talk without your child over-hearing. Talk about problems that have come up, schedule changes that need to be made, reactions your child is having and things coming up in the future.

If child support needs to be discussed, do so either at the end of the meeting or at an entirely different time.

Speak calmly and rationally, pushing aside all of those emotions that will get in the way of your objective.

The need for such formal meetings will dissipate the longer you are divorced and you will eventually learn to have quick unscheduled phone calls or chats. There may be times when large problems develop in the future and you find that resuming a regular meeting or phone call schedule can help.

Getting Help

If you are having trouble communicating with each other (after all, old habits are hard to break), consider seeing a mediator who can help you work through the issues and develop a new way to talk to each other without arguments. It really is possible to do so.

Your local bar association or the Academy of Family Mediators (781-674-2663, **http://www.mediators.org**) can help you find a media-tor. A mediator acts as a neutral third party who helps you and the other parent work through problems yourselves. If you and the other parent find you are completely unable to solve visitation problems, a mediator can help solve the problems at hand and teach you how to resolve problems that may arise in the future.

When All Else Fails:
Try the Business Transaction Approach

If you have tried working together, if you have tried biting your tongue and none of it has worked, if you and the other parent are at each other's throats and can't agree on anything, think of your dealings with him or her as a business transaction. Be polite, but do not argue or dis-play emotion. Communicate by written notes if you can't talk. You want to accomplish the task of arranging visitation and exchanging your child. Remember that is not about you, your feelings or the way you deserve to be treated. This is about making sure your child has two par-ents. Treat the situation as one you just need to deal with as you would any other kind of activity in your daily life.

You might have a cranky cashier at the grocery store, and while this behavior is not appropriate or polite, you somehow find a way to deal with it so you can get your groceries. View this situation in the same light. You have a goal you want to accomplish (making sure your child has relationships with two parents) and the way to accomplish it is to keep your feelings to yourself and just get through the situation. Arranging and facilitating regular visitation is part of your responsibilities as a parent.

When It Is Unbearable

You and the other parent may be at the point where you absolutely despise each other and the thought of being polite to him or her may make you cringe. You don't have to be best buddies, you just have to find a way to communicate about visitation without screaming at each other.

If you feel that you and the other parent simply cannot communicate at all at this point, you probably need a break from each other. Have your child ready for scheduled visits, deal with the transfer and simply do not talk to the other parent beyond the essentials. If you can't even handle this, then ask a friend or relative to help you with the transfers. Let your best friend or sister open the door and make sure all of the child's belongings go with the child. If you need to avoid contact for a while, it's ok. It will probably ease the tension if you avoid each other for a while. It takes a while for emotions to simmer down after a divorce or separation. Most likely, things will eventually improve to the point where you can exchange your child without too much discomfort. But, this may take time and you need to patient. You can't decide you want to end visitation because it is too uncomfortable for you. It's important for your child. Even if your child does not seem to have a very good relationship with the other parent right now, you have to give them the opportunity to know each other and be together.

Developing a good parenting partnership can take time. You can't go directly from the heat of a nasty custody battle to cooperating fully with each other the next day. This is something you need to gradually build up to. Take baby steps if you need to. Here are some tips to remember when communicating with the other parent:

> *Do not yell.* The best way to communicate with the other parent is by using a neutral, calm voice. Raising your voice will lead to an argument.

> *Be clear about what you are talking about.* Try to address only one issue at a time. Do not confuse things by bringing up other topics or problems.

➤ *Let the past go*. Don't try to discuss what has happened in the past with your relationship. Focus on the present and the future with regard to your child.

➤ *Repeat yourself if necessary*. Sometimes you may try to discuss an issue relating to visitation and the other parent will try to bring up other things—child support, arguments over possessions, etc. If you respond, you will both be diverted from the important issue at hand—visitation. Repeat your question or comment calmly until he or she answers it. You can also say that you are not willing to talk about the other issue now and want only to talk about the visitation issue.

➤ *Choose your times*. If you want to have a discussion with the other parent, do so at a time when you are both able to talk freely and are not rushed or tired.

➤ *Try to talk in "I" phrases instead of "you" phrases*. If you are having a problem with visitation, say things like, "I am having trouble picking Trevor up at 4 P.M. Could we change it to 5 P.M.?" Avoid saying things like, "You are going to have to change the time we exchange Trevor." Try to focus the sentence on *your* needs, *your* problem, *your* situation and avoid sentences that sound like accusations, criticisms or complaints.

➤ *Don't discuss things you don't need to*. This means letting some things go and focusing on the important issues. Do you really need to discuss whether your child watched TV after 9 P.M. at the other parent's house? Probably not, unless there is an ongoing problem. Choose your issues and let the smaller ones go.

➤ *Speak with respect*. Remember, he or she is your child's other parent and is extremely important to your child. This is the person you created life with. He or she deserves to be treated with respect, even if you believe that he or she is truly not worthy of it.

7

THE SINGLE PARENT LIFE

Now that you are through the separation or divorce, it is time for you to look forward. You have a parenting plan that you need to follow and you need to find a way to make it a part of your life and your child's life. You need to move on with your own life, but you need to make sure you consider your child's needs when you do so. You are in a delicate period where you have a lot of decisions to make. You are living alone as a single parent for the first time and you need to find a way to create a life that will be comfortable for both you and your child. Be aware that there will also be times in the future when you will find you have to readjust your priorities, your plans, and your lifestyle as your child grows older and as different situations develop. Come back to this chapter then for help.

Coping with the Changes

Dealing with the divorce or separation and the change in living arrangements was difficult and it seems like things should get easier now. Things will probably just be different. There are going to be bumps along the road as you, your child, and the other parent adjust to the new order of things. There will be times when you are angry that you have to deal with your child alone, times when you will be angry at the other parent for butting in and times when nothing seems like it will ever be right again. All of this is natural and it is important that you do the best you can under the circumstances. No one's perfect, no one's life is perfect and nobody makes the right decisions all the time. So pick yourself up and move forward, doing the best you can at the time. You are a good parent and a good person, and you can move forward.

Running a House Alone

So here you are, a single parent, with a house and family to manage. This can seem overwhelming. However, you managed all of these things when you and the other parent were still together so you can continue to do so. Some things will actually be easier because there won't be any arguing or compromising involved. You can do things your way. Some things will be difficult as you find yourself learning to do the things around the house that the other parent used to take care of.

You have to make your own routine, your own rules and your own plan for living as a single parent. While the thought of suddenly being in charge of the entire household may seem overwhelming, try to take things one at a time. If you sit down and try to face all of your decisions, responsibilities and changes at once, it is overwhelming. Try coping with one problem or task at a time. Soon you will find that you are getting into a routine and it doesn't seem so frightening. It can also be helpful to make lists. Make a list of everything that needs to be done this week, and then one for everything that needs to be done today. Work on one item on the list at a time. Use a calendar so you can keep track of you commitments, your child's commitments, as well as the visitation schedule.

Making Decisions

Don't make any radical decisions right away—such as moving, spending a lot of money on household purchases, etc. Give yourself time to adjust to the new situation. When it's time to make big decisions, you'll know and you will find freedom and joy in doing so.

Expect changes and decisions to be difficult for your child as well. Certainly things are going to be topsy turvy for a while, but everyone in the household will get used to them. You are the parent and you will be making the big decisions. Your child's input should be welcome, but not decisive. *Everyone* is adjusting and you and your child have to make some of these adjustments together.

Having a Life

It is important that you continue to have your job, friends, family and hobbies. These are the things that make you a well-rounded person and help you cope with stress. Don't give up the things that are important to you. Parenting is important, but it should not be your entire life. Find a way to balance your needs with those of your child. Continue to be your own person with your own passions and interests. Show your child how important it is to go on living.

Scheduling

Now that a parenting plan is such a big part of your life, it's important to give it priority. You are going to have to get used to living and dying by the schedule. It is especially important in the first few months after a divorce or separation to follow your schedule closely so that your child can adjust to it. It will feel like an imposition to have the schedule infringe upon your new freedom, but remember that all you are doing is making sure your child has time with the other parent, which is a reasonable thing to do. The schedule is a tool that helps divide your child's time. It really isn't a cross to bear or a ball and chain. Think of it as your child's time that is being shared. Of course, your child wants to share time with both parents. Respect the schedule the same way you respect this sentiment.

Parenting Alone

If you have a typical parenting plan, you will be parenting alone for long stretches of time. When you look at the calendar and see stretches of four, five, nine or twelve days when you will be parenting alone, it may feel overwhelming. But remember you only have to deal with one day at a time!

Remember that you are your child's parent, you have been successfully parenting throughout your child's life and your parenting skills are good—otherwise the court would not have placed you in this situation.

Accept that you aren't going to be perfect at single parenting. Everyone makes mistakes. Do the best you can at this difficult job.

You Don't Have to Do This Alone

If you need help, ask for it. You don't have to be a super parent. Call on your family and close friends to help you. You may find you are facing jobs or tasks around the house the other parent always did and you are not skilled at. Ask for help and learn how to do them so you can become self-sufficient.

Ask for family and friends to babysit or do things with your child. Do not be afraid to ask the other parent to help. If you need a babysitter, see if he or she is available. Ask the other parent to handle some things—taking your child to the doctor, for a haircut, shopping for new shoes, to a school activity or on outings with the child's friends. Doing so will give you a break, help the other parent feel involved and important and let your child know he or she still has two parents who take responsibility for him or her. It's OK to have time by yourself!

Look through the list of resources in Appendix B at the end of this book to find organizations, web sites, and books that can provide you with additional support. Here are some ways for managing as a single parent:

➤ Take things one day at a time.

➤ Don't expect to be perfect.

➤ Ask for help from family, friends and the other parent.

➤ Continue to have friends and activities that make you happy.

➤ Don't be afraid of being alone and take some time to get used to it.

➤ Make 'to do' lists to help you get organized around the house.

➤ Use a calendar to stay organized.

➤ Remember that your child is adjusting to things, just as you are.

➤ Don't take on too much or over schedule yourself out of the fear of being lonely.

➤ Make time for your child.

➤ Include your child in some decisions around the house. Keep him or her involved in daily family life.

➤ Don't make drastic changes too soon; take time to decide what will be best for you and your child.

➤ Remember that you are not doing anything new, you're just doing it in a different way. You will be able to cope.

8

ENCOURAGING AND ASSISTING WITH VISITATION

You may feel that in many ways your hard work is done. You survived the separation or divorce and negotiated the court system so that your child would live primarily with you. You take the time to make sure you have a good relationship with your child and anything the other parent does or doesn't do isn't your problem.

Actually, this really isn't the case. You do need to be involved with visitation and your child's relationship with the other parent to make sure that your child is able to handle it and get the benefits from it.

You may feel that you are the parent who is most responsible for your child and that you are the one who is best suited to care for your child. If this is the case, then isn't it part of your responsibility to make sure your child maintains a healthy relationship with the other parent? If you felt that your child was not maintaining a healthy relationship with a grandparent, you would make some effort to improve it, wouldn't you? If you truly feel that you are the most responsible parent, then it is part of your responsibility to make sure your child continues to have a good relationship with the other parent. This means you need to encourage visitation.

If you feel that the other parent is a reasonably good parent and it is important to you that you share responsibility for your child, then it is equally important that you encourage your child to see the other parent and spend time with him or her. If you feel the other parent is not the greatest parent, it is even more important that you support and encourage visitation since he or she may not be completely on top of it. Your child lives with you most of the time and part of your responsibility as a custodial parent is making sure that he or she continues to have a second parent and benefit from that relationship.

Talking to Your Child About Visitation

The one thing to remember when communicating with your child, verbally and nonverbally, is that you must be positive and encouraging about the time he or she spends with the other parent. It is easy to remember to only say positive things. It is difficult to stop yourself from displaying your resentment, anger or hurt in nonverbal ways. Your actions convey as much information as your words. If you slam the door when the other parent leaves, speak to him or her in a hostile voice, or allow your body language to convey your anger, this information will get through to your child and inform him or her that you really wish he or she wasn't spending time with the other parent. This is hurtful and confusing to children and teens alike.

Sometimes children act as if they do not want to go with the other parent. Your job is to make sure that they do. Sometimes children act as if they can't stand you and can't wait to get away from you. Your job is not show any resentment or anger about this. You are, of course, going to have emotional reactions to these two situations, but what you need to focus on is that your child needs to see the other parent and it is important that you put your stamp of approval on the entire situation. Your feelings are valid, but they should not enter into the visitation equation.

THINGS TO SAY ABOUT VISITATION

- ➤ It is important to me that you spend time with your mom/dad.
- ➤ I want you to spend time with Mom/Dad because she/he is your other parent and that will never change.
- ➤ Yes, I'll miss you, but I'm glad you'll have some time with Mom/Dad.
- ➤ Have fun! See you when you come home.
- ➤ I'm sorry you don't feel like going, but today is your day to be with Mom/Dad.
- ➤ He/She will always be your mom/dad and I wouldn't have it any other way.

THINGS *NOT* TO SAY ABOUT VISITATION

➤ I wish I could go, too.
➤ Well, I guess you'll just have to miss the big family reunion at the beach since you'll be with Mom/Dad. Too bad.
➤ You'd rather be with him/her anyhow, so just go.
➤ Wouldn't you rather just stay here with me and rent a movie?
➤ I am so nervous when you are alone with him/her.
➤ I don't know why you want to go with him/her.

Children easily pick up on your emotional state, so you have got to find a way to suppress it if what you feel is going to make your child uncomfortable about spending time with the other parent. This does not mean you can't have those feelings. The key is not to show them around your child if possible.

Your Responsibility for Visitation

When the court gave you custody of your child, the judge also gave you the responsibility for making sure your child continued to see the other parent and have the other parent in his or her life. In fact, if you interfere with or try to avoid visitation, this can be the basis for a change of custody. You cannot wipe your hands and walk away saying to the other parent, "You're on your own—good luck!" You have a responsibility to make sure that visitation is a priority in your child's life. Do not schedule your child for a regular activity on the other parent's day without discussing it with him or her or seeing what arrangements can be made. Make sure you emphasize to your child that visitation is important and something that must be given priority in his or her life.

It is also important to remember that you are not solely in charge in your child's life. The other parent is part of your child's life and it is essential that all of you continue to act as if he or she has an important role.

When Your Child Does Not Want to Go Visit

Most children reach a point where one day they say that they do not want to go on visitation. Visitation is not optional for your child, just as it is not optional for you. Spending time with one's parents is a lifelong commitment. When your children are adults, they can decide for themselves if they wish to continue their relationships with their parents. While they are children they do not have this choice. You are the parent and you must make sure that your child follows the rules that have been created for your family. Furthermore, you have been ordered by the court to allow visitation at scheduled times. If you do not, you are violating a court order and can be held in contempt of court, which can mean jail time and fines, not to mention the fact that you could lose custody.

When the day comes when your child refuses to go, you are responsible for making sure he or she goes. It is your legal duty. Of course, it is not easy to convince a child to do something he or she is opposed to, but you can get this done in the same way you get your child to clean his room, go to the store with you, go to the dentist or do anything else that he or she refuses to do. Take away privileges, take away cherished items, and so on. Use the discipline techniques that are effective with your child (note: physical punishment is never an effective discipline technique and should never be used). It is important to remain calm when this happens. Screaming and yelling are not going to improve the situation.

It is important that you and the other parent present a united front on this matter. You must both act as if the scheduled time is going to happen and you must not give in. If you give in and allow your child to stay home with you once, it becomes clear to the child that he can play one of you off the other, that you don't mean what you say and that you are not serious about how important time with the other parent is. It also becomes clear to the other parent that you are not working with him or her and are trying to undercut him or her and find ways out of the schedule you both agreed to. In short, giving in will negatively affect all of you. If you think that you "win" by keeping your child home, you are mistaken. You are telling your child that you don't think the relationship with the other parent is important. You are helping your child push away the other parent. You are effectively denying your child his or her right to have two parents that love and care for him or her—through good times and bad times.

When Your Child Would Rather Be There

Just as there are times when your child will refuse to go on visitation, there will be times when he or she will not want to come home or will make noise about preferring to be with the other parent. All of this is normal and it is something you just have to get through. Of course, this is going to hurt your feelings. Your feelings would have been hurt before the divorce or separation if your child had refused to spend time with you then. Don't get hung up on this. Remember that children rebel and it is natural and normal. Just as you did when your child refused to go on visitation, you have to stick to your guns and to your schedule. Children do not get to choose where they live and which parent they would rather be with. You and the other parent must make sure your child understands that you both will always listen to what he or she has to say, but that the parents are the ones who make the decisions about living arrangements.

Your time with your child is just as important as the other parent's time with your child and it is important that you support each other and stand by the schedule.

All that being said, there are circumstances where a change of custody would be the best thing for a child. It is common for teens to have a real need to spend more time with the parent of the same sex. Should it become clear that your child truly wants and needs to live with the other parent, you, the other parent and the child need to discuss this, and you may need to talk to your lawyer. It may be a good idea to talk with a family therapist or counselor to find out if this is really what is best for your child. It would be up to the other parent to file court papers seeking a change in custody at this point.

Transitions

For most children, the transition from one parent to another is the most difficult part of visitation. When your child goes from one parent to the other, expect there to be some difficulties. To make transitions easier when your child is returned to you, you should talk about what you have planned and what you will be doing that day. When the child is going to the other parent, talk about what he or she will be doing with the other parent and when he or she will see you next.

Many parents find that the most difficult part of time with their children is the time at the beginning and end of their scheduled time. It is hard for children to leave one parent and instantly get into the groove with the other. When your child comes home, give each other a little space to adjust without immediately jumping into an intense activity together. Allow your child time to unpack or get a snack if you are at home or time to adjust to the surroundings if you are in public.

Teens also have problems transitioning and may be moody, silent, or hostile. Give your teen space and time to adjust. To ease the transition to the other parent, tell your child in advance when he or she will go with the other parent and give some additional reminders, such as two hours before, one hour before and half an hour before. Make sure when you part that you are able to point to the next time you will be together and make some reference to what you will be doing together then. Also point out if you will have phone or email contact before then.

Some parents find that transitions can be eased if the parent the child is currently with transports the child to the other parent. So, the other parent would bring the child home to you and you would take the child to the other parent's house. Transitioning in a public place such as a park, a mall, or a restaurant, can make things easier. It may also be easier if you do not transition directly with the other parent. He or she could pick your child up at school and return him or her there the next school morning. In some situations, a child may do better with transitions if another adult is involved. For example, the child could be dropped off and picked up at a grandparent's house. Here are some other ways to ease transitions:

- Transition in a public place if necessary.
- Use school beginning or ending as a transition time so the child does not go directly from one parent to the other.
- Transition at a neutral place, such as a relative's home.
- Don't shoehorn your child from one parent's car to the other's. Spend a few minutes somewhere before popping him or her back in a car.
- Tell your child a joke or a funny story or do something to lighten the mood.
- Remind him or her when you will be together again or if it is the beginning of your time, remind him or her when he or she will be with the other parent next.
- Give him or her some space to adjust. Allow some quiet individual time if you are at home before getting into an activity together.
- Keep your thoughts or complaints about the other parent under wraps.
- Don't try to use transition time as a time to discuss big issues with your child.
- Be polite and friendly to the other parent. Smile!
- Try not to rush. Being frantic just makes things worse.
- If hugging and kissing is natural for you, do it!
- Make it clear you are happy to see your child when your time together begins.
- Don't act sad or upset when your child is leaving you. It's OK to feel this way, but don't burden your child with this.
- Don't try to get your child to hide or suppress feelings of sadness or anger. Work on helping him or her through it.
- Use distraction to get your child thinking about something else.

Helping Your Child With Long Distance Visitation

If the other parent lives far away, you need to develop some strategies for helping your child cope with long distance visitation.

Even though your child is physically separated from the other parent, this does not mean they have to be out of touch or emotionally separated. Encourage your child and the other parent to share regular phone calls. If the other parent cannot handle the expense, maybe you could share the cost. You can also encourage people to give your child phone call gift cards.

Encourage them to send each other letters and packages. Set up an email account for your child or use an online instant messenger program so that the child and other parent can communicate quickly and easily. They can send each other faxes, post things on a private website or see each other via web cams. There are also computer games you can buy, such as JumpStart Baby (from The Learning Company), that allow the child and other parent to play a computer game together over the Internet. Take photos your child can send to the other parent. Send copies of report cards and videotapes of recitals.

When the other parent and your child do see each other in person, it will be need to be in bigger chunks of time than the typical visitation schedule. If your child is very young, it makes more sense for the other parent to come to your area so that the child can continue to have time with both parents. As a child grows, he or she will be able to visit the other parent out of town. Think about how you will arrange transportation. Perhaps one of you could drive the child there and the other parent could drive the child home. Some parents are comfortable allowing their children to fly alone and airlines can make accommodations for this so that an employee will escort the child.

While your child is away with the other parent, make sure that you have frequent telephone and/or email contact so that the child knows you are still accessible to him or her.

Vacations

When your child vacations with you or with the other parent, it is important that you and the other parent share phone numbers and itineraries with each other. Children should be able to have phone contact with the parent they are away from.

Coping With All That "Stuff"

One of the main things parents argue about is their child's belongings. "You didn't send any clean underwear," "How could you forget to bring his soccer uniform back?" or "What do you mean you can't find the pacifier?" Dealing with your child's "stuff" is one of the biggest difficulties you may have to cope with.

It is a good idea to set some ground rules about the belongings. There are some items that will need to travel with the child, such as school books, instruments, sports equipment, special toys or blankies, coats and shoes. It is best if the other parent is encouraged to provide some items that can stay at his or her home. He or she can purchase some clothes, toys, books, and so on to keep at his or her home, or maybe there some items you are willing to send from your home that can stay at the other home. This will reduce the amount of items being exchanged.

Laundry is a heated point of contention with some parents. The best policy is to return the clothes that belong at the other house laundered, if there is time. Discuss this with the other parent. Older children can take on this responsibility themselves.

Develop a system for making sure the right items go with your child on visitation. It may be helpful to post a list on your refrigerator or bulletin board so that nothing is forgotten while packing. In the beginning you will need to assist with packing. It will take a while for your child to get into the swing of this. Children over age 8 should be encouraged to eventually manage their belongings themselves.

If your child returns home and essential items are missing, you will need to contact the other parent and arrange for him or her to drop them off or for you to go pick them up. Encourage the other parent to use a list to keep track of what needs to come home. You can also send a checklist of everything you have packed if you think this will help. You may wish to use a marker chart so the list can remain permanent. You can mark items off each time in erasable marker.

SAMPLE LIST OF BELONGINGS THAT TRAVEL FOR AN INFANT OR TODDLER

- ❏ snowsuit/coat
- ❏ clothes
- ❏ blanket
- ❏ pacifier
- ❏ special toys
- ❏ medication
- ❏ any bottles, cups or dishes that came with the child
- ❏ diaper bag

SAMPLE LIST OF BELONGINGS THAT TRAVEL FOR A SCHOOL AGE CHILD:

- ❑ backpack
- ❑ homework
- ❑ books
- ❑ sneakers
- ❑ bag of clothes
- ❑ sports uniform/equipment
- ❑ computer disks (for homework)
- ❑ assignment notebook
- ❑ stuffed animal or action figures
- ❑ instrument
- ❑ hand-held video games
- ❑ favorite pillow
- ❑ lunchbox
- ❑ coat
- ❑ boots/shoes
- ❑ medication
- ❑ laminated card with both parents' phone numbers, cell phone number, pagers and email addresses

SAMPLE LIST OF BELONGINGS THAT TRAVEL FOR A TEEN:

- ❑ cosmetics and other hygiene items that he or she is particular about
- ❑ hair brush
- ❑ personal CD player
- ❑ CDs
- ❑ computer disks and games
- ❑ homework and school books
- ❑ backpack
- ❑ coat
- ❑ cheerleader outfit/sport uniform and equipment
- ❑ diary or journal
- ❑ boots/shoes
- ❑ bag of clothes and accessories
- ❑ cell phone
- ❑ medication
- ❑ personal organizer
- ❑ instrument
- ❑ laptop
- ❑ wallet or purse

Medication

Always send instructions if you are sending medication with your child and ask that the other parent keep track of when doses are given. It may be helpful to enclose a dosage chart for the other parent to fill in. Ask him or her to record all prescription and non-prescription medications that are given. Explain that it is important for you to know when medicine was given so that you can give the next dose on time. In return, you must let the other parent know when you last gave medication, so he or she can determine when to give the next dose. Do so by entering this on the top line of the dosage chart. If you have a chronically ill child, it is a good idea to have the other parent talk to the doctor at some point to review medications and treatment.

SAMPLE DOSAGE CHART			
Date	Time	Name of medication	Amount Given
___	___	___	___
___	___	___	___
___	___	___	___
___	___	___	___
___	___	___	___
___	___	___	___

9

HOLIDAYS

Holidays are a very emotional time for divorced or separated people. They are even more difficult when children are in the equation. Your heart may ache at the thought of being apart from your child during part of a holiday. Holidays are also difficult for the children of separation or divorce. Children are sad and angry that both parents are not there. They are also sure they are hurting the parent they are not with. Try to remember how difficult the situation is for your child and for the other parent. You need to realize that holidays will always have to be shared in some way from now on and neither parent is going to get to see the child on every holiday. Problems with holidays may pop up again in the future, so refer back to this chapter when needed.

Being Realistic

Whatever great or awful things you expect a holiday to bring, you are probably wrong! Expect it to be good and bad, but not the picture perfect festival or the absolute lonely disaster you are envisioning. Be realistic about your expectations to yourself and to your child. View the holiday as another day that may have some nice components or some sad components to it.

Before a holiday comes around, take some time to talk about it with your child. Discuss whose house he or she will be at. Talk about how you both feel about the plans. Let your child tell you what he or she likes or dislikes about the plan. Think of what you, your child and the other parent can do to make the holiday go well.

The best way to ensure that a holiday will go well is to think about giving your child the gift of happiness and love. You can give these things to your child no matter where he or she is. Focus on the joy a child deserves to experience, not on the loss or anger you feel. Let your child know that you love her and want her to have a good holiday, no matter where she is each year.

Holidays *with* Your Child

When it is your turn to have your child for an important holiday, do not expect it to be of storybook quality. Be prepared for your child to miss the other parent. Discuss what you and your child will be doing and make sure there is some time built into the schedule for a phone call between your child and the other parent and possibly the other grandparents. Drop a hint to the other parent that he or she should call the child if you think he or she won't think of it. It will be natural for your child to miss them and a phone call will help make contact again. Get your child involved in your holiday plans and preparations.

Your visitation schedule probably has your child with the appropriate parent on Mother's Day or Father's Day. Enjoy your day and focus on your relationship with your son or daughter. That's what the day is all about after all. Think of this as a day for celebrating motherhood or fatherhood and all the joys it has brought you. Encourage your child to make a card or gift for the other parent's day and make sure that they see, or at least talk, to each other.

Holidays *without* Your Child

It is easy to get wrapped up in the pain of spending a holiday alone. It is normal to feel abandoned, left out and angry when you are unable to spend a holiday with your child. You need to find some way to get yourself through the day.

Find some way to be good to yourself that day. Feel free to acknowledge your feelings of sadness, anger, loss and grief. Go ahead and wallow, cry or yell. Your feelings are real and cannot be pushed aside.

Next, think about your child. Try to arrange for some telephone contact on the holiday. Touching base will make you both feel better. It is OK to tell your child how much you miss him or her, but do not make him or her feel sorry for you or guilty. Give your child permission to enjoy the day without you. ("Have a good time at Grandma's house!" or "Have a great time opening those presents!")

If you haven't already done so, schedule an alternate time for you to celebrate the holiday with your child, such as the next day or when the child returns to your home. Remind your child of this during your phone call. Celebrate when you are next together. Even though it won't technically be the holiday, it can be *your* holiday. If you and the other parent are alternating holidays, remind yourself and your child that next year you will be together for this holiday.

When you talk to your child or see him or her afterwards, let him or her tell you about how he or she spent the holiday. Try to just listen without criticizing or making judgments. Comments like, "Your grandfather always lets you eat too much candy," will ruin your child's joy in the event. Be positive and let your child know you are happy he or she had a good day ("I'm glad you got that bicycle you've been wishing for!").

Some ideas for handling a holiday alone are:
- ➤ spend time with friends or family
- ➤ attend a religious service if it is part of how you celebrate
- ➤ invite some people to a gathering at your home
- ➤ donate your time that day to a charity
- ➤ go to a movie and splurge on popcorn and candy
- ➤ rent a video
- ➤ curl up with a good book
- ➤ work on a home improvement project
- ➤ organize your photographs
- ➤ take a walk
- ➤ buy yourself a gift
- ➤ go to a parade, fireworks or other community event
- ➤ cook yourself a special holiday meal
- ➤ clean your closets
- ➤ build a dollhouse or racetrack for your child
- ➤ rearrange the furniture
- ➤ visit an Internet chat room and talk to other parents in the same situation
- ➤ sleep in and eat breakfast in bed
- ➤ go away on a trip by yourself
- ➤ get that project done for work that you've been putting off
- ➤ go to a museum
- ➤ plant a garden
- ➤ take the time to start a hobby you've never tried
- ➤ perform a random act of kindness for a stranger
- ➤ go to the gym
- ➤ eat junk food

HOLIDAY TRAPS TO AVOID

- ➤ making plans for every second. Leave some down time for you and your child to spend together, or for your child to decompress alone.
- ➤ being overly gay and festive. Of course you want to make the day special and you want your child to have fun, but too much gaiety can seem false. You also run the risk of making your child feel bad for not being equally thrilled.
- ➤ trying to follow the exact same traditions you used to follow as a family. Nothing can ever truly be as it was and you only bring up bittersweet memories for both of you by trying to recreate the past.
- ➤ completely reinventing the holiday. Your child will want some things to be familiar and traditional. Pick some of the things you used to do as a family and incorporate them with some of your own new traditions to make it a special day.
- ➤ surrounding yourself with too many people. You don't want your child to get lost in a crowd. Schedule some alone time.
- ➤ isolating yourselves. If part of your holiday tradition involves visiting other family members, continue to do so. Focusing all of your time and attention on your child is too much pressure.
- ➤ doing the "remember when" routine. A big part of holidays has to do with memories. It is OK to talk about a few things from the past, but in general, try to look forward. Constant reminiscing could easily make you both sad or angry if you dwell on it.
- ➤ becoming depressed. It is natural for both you and your child to feel sad or angry because divorce or separation has changed your family. It is OK to be honest with your child ("It feels strange to me too not to have Daddy here"), but you should not unload your emotions ("I feel so alone because Mommy doesn't love me anymore"). Acknowledging the changed situation is OK, but dwelling on it is not.

Sharing Holidays

Many families find that in the first few years after a divorce or separation, the children are happiest if they can spend some time with their parents together on holidays. Some families spend part of Christmas morning together or share Thanksgiving dinner. If this is something you would like to do, discuss it with the other parent. You must both be comfortable and willing to make an arrangement like this work. If you do decide to try it, remember to keep things light. An argument will ruin the day.

Gifts

Gift-giving can easily turn into a competition between parents. Each tries to give better, more expensive presents to prove he or she is the better parent. The best way to avoid this is to discuss it with the other parent. Some parents agree to discuss any purchases over $100 with each other. Other parents give each other ideas about what each is buying so that there is little duplication. Others agree on a total amount each will not exceed. Like everything else involved with parenting, things always work best when there is communication between the parents. Some parents even give some big important gifts together. Whatever works in your situation is OK.

Avoid showering your child with gifts to make up for the time you spend apart. This strategy really does not work. Think about the amount and type of gifts your child received before the divorce. Try to stick to the same plan.

All of this does not mean that you cannot buy your child that computer, video game system, or puppy he or she has been begging for. Try to discuss your plans with the other parent. If it is something your child really wants, it is unlikely the other parent will object, as long as he or she is not blindsided with it when the gift is given.

Where will your child keep the gifts you give him or her? You should decide ahead of time if you want the item to stay at your home or if your child can decide where to keep it.

Although it is unlikely you and the other parent will exchange gifts, your child certainly will want to give the other parent a gift. You could take him or her shopping and let him or her buy a gift for the other parent or encourage a teen to do so. While you may have bad feelings toward the other parent, remember that your child loves him or her and sharing in the gift-giving will make your child feel happy. If you absolutely are not comfortable helping your child do this, try to see if some other family member can make sure your child has the opportunity to shop for both parents. With pre-teen or teen aged children, the child can do the shopping if transportation is arranged, but may need a reminder about getting a gift for the other parent.

Birthdays

You may not see your child on his or her birthday because you and the other parent have agreed to alternate the day or because it falls on a day when the child is with the other parent. Make contact with your child on the birthday—a phone call or a quick stop at the front door for a hug.

Celebrate at the next opportunity. This is your child's special day. Do not let your problems with the other parent affect it! If the child is with you, make sure he or she has the opportunity to take a call from the other parent. You might want to hint to the other parent that a phone call would help make the day special.

Some parents have a policy of having both parents present at birthday parties. If you and the other parent are both comfortable with this, give it a try.

Final Thoughts

Attorneys know there is generally an increase in visitation disputes at holiday times. Attorneys find themselves flooded with calls on the day before Thanksgiving, Christmas Eve, etc. Don't be one of the phone calls if you can help it. Don't let the holidays derail you. Constant court battles are usually not the answer. Find a way to work things out with the other parent. If you need help dealing with your emotions, see a counselor or therapist. Clergy are also experienced in dealing with holiday emotions and disputes. Do whatever you have to do to get through holidays. Remember that they do come every year, so it is not the end of the world if you have a disappointing experience this year.

10

DEALING WITH
SCHEDULES

One of the hardest things to deal with once you are divorced or separated is learning to live with the parenting schedule. Parenting on a schedule is a learned skill. You're used to your child being at home whenever you are and being free to go anywhere when you go. Things are different now and although your child is the one who is going to be spending time with the other parent, you are the one who is going to have to make this schedule a part of both your lives.

The Schedule

Most families have a schedule that is set by the court or agreed to by both parents. This schedule can be adjusted if both you and the other parent agree to alter it. Once the schedule is set, it is important that both you, the other parent and your child have it on a calendar. There is nothing worse than forgetting to have your child ready for visitation or forgetting to be home on time for your child's return because you got your days mixed up. You will disappoint your child.

You also need to help your child learn to live by the schedule. Create a calendar for the child with the schedule clearly marked. For young children, a color-coded calendar is very helpful. Color Mom's days blue and Dad's days red (or any other color you choose) and on the transition days, split the day in half with a color on each side. This visual aid will assist younger children in seeing where they will be on each day and will help prepare them for the transitions. Older children can use a calendar that has pick-up and drop-off times written on it. Teens may wish to incorporate the schedule into their school calendar or on their computers or organizers.

When you create a schedule, it is a good idea to have some basic schedule rules in place, such as whoever is with the child at 6 P.M. will feed him or her dinner or whoever is with the child until 8 P.M at night will assist with homework. These basic rules will allow you to avoid having discussions and negotiations about these basic daily events.

SAMPLE SCHEDULING RULES

> Changes to the schedule require a 24 hour notice, except in emergencies.

> The parents will try to accommodate reasonable schedule change requests made by each other.

> If the parent providing transportation will be late, he or she will call as soon as possible to let the other parent and child know.

> Each parent will be assigned pick-up and drop-off duties that will remain the same. Pick-ups and drop-offs will be at a set time; for example, Parent A will always drop off the child at 7 P.M. every other Friday, and Parent B will always drop off the child at 2 P.M. every other Sunday. These times will not change unless the parents agree.

> The parents will meet or talk once a month to exchange scheduling information.

> The non-custodial parent will contact the school and extra-curricular activities leaders for copies of calendars and schedules. If a calendar change notice is sent home with the child, it will be shared with the non-custodial parent.

> Schedule change requests will be made directly by one parent to the other and messages will not be carried by the child.

> If the child has a scheduled activity planned during visitation, the non-custodial parent will transport the child (if needed) to and from the activity.

> The non-custodial parent shall have the right to have the child skip a normally planned activity scheduled during his or her visitation time if he or she has a more important, one-time event planned.

> Each parent will maintain a calendar and keep track of visitation times and the child's activities.

> An age appropriate calendar will be maintained for the child's use.

Understanding Your Child's Schedule

It is important for you to remember that your child has a schedule of his or her own. Many children and teens (see Chapters 12 and 13 for more information about teens) participate in after school activities and have various lessons and classes to attend. You need to obtain copies of all correspondence that deals with your child's schedule. Make sure these notices do not get left in your child's backpack or bag. It is also important that the other parent be familiar with your child's schedule. Suggest to the other parent that he or she request that the school, coach, group leader, etc. copy him or her on all correspondence. He or she can obtain a copy of the school calendar from the main office. It's also important to remember that some of this information is usually just sent home with the child. You and the other parent need to agree that whoever receives this information should share it with the other parent. If your child is picked up at school by the other parent and has an important scheduling notice sent home that day, make sure that a system is in place so that both parents will be made aware of it.

Make sure you obtain a copy of the school calendar as well as notifications about field trips and other special events. Mark all of these on your calendar, even if they are happening on a day when you won't be with your child (your parenting schedule could change and you might need this information). It is in your best interest to make sure the other parent is aware of things that are on the calendar, so try to keep him or her up to date.

Dealing with Conflicts

Many parents feel torn when faced with a conflict between visitation time and a scheduled activity of the child's. Think about these situations in this way. When all of you lived together in one home, did your child have to skip the prom or a soccer game because one of you wanted to spend time with him or her? You or your spouse took the child to the event (or saw him or her before and afterwards) and fit in family time around it. This is how life should continue. You need to continue to allow your child to participate in activities that are important to him or her. If you or the other parent constantly require a child to skip activities, all you will get out of it will be resentment. If your child has an event planned on the same night he or she is supposed to spend the evening with the other parent, see if it can be arranged for the other parent to take the child to and from the activity and fit in some family time before or after it. The same goes for your time with your child. Do the best you can to get your child to his or her scheduled events. You should never, ever place your child in the position of having to choose between visitation and an activity that is important to him or her. There will be times when there are conflicts and you will have to make a decision at that time where the child will go, but remember that this is a decision for the parents to make and not the child. Children should not be asked to choose between their parents and their friends or activities.

If you find that there are too many ongoing conflicts with visitation, then you and the other parent need to rearrange the schedule to take into consideration the child's schedule.

When to Say No

Although it is important for your child to continue in sports and activities that are fun and enriching, there does come a time when you should say no. If your child is scheduled for something every single day, it might be time to talk to the child about cutting back. If you and your child or the other parent and the child have something important planned (such as a camping trip together or your grandmother's 90th birthday party) that conflicts with a planned activity, you are using your authority as a parent when you decide the child will have to miss the activity just this once. Be sure to explain this calmly to your child. The other parent might have something important planned together that might necessitate missing one of the child's activities sometime as well.

Your Child's Friends

Friends aren't a big issue for children under 5. When kids reach elementary school, friends become more important. Encourage your child to invite friends to your home. Suggest that the other parent invite some of the child's friends over once in a while. Continuing to see friends at both homes will help your child adjust to the new life and help him or her maintain the friendships that are so important. It's also fine for your child to have some playdates or time at a friend's home during his or her time with the other parent. It will be up to the other parent to agree to this. You should not plan these get-togethers. Tell your child to discuss this with the other parent. Teens are another story entirely. See Chapter 13 for more information about dealing with teens and their friends.

Changing Your Schedule

There may come a time when you find that you do not have enough time with your child. Perhaps you are working a strange schedule or your child is with the other parent on all of your free days. Part of being a parent is spending time with your child. If you find that this is not happening, maybe some changes need to be made. Talk to the other parent about changing when visitation takes place. Look at your child's schedule to see if perhaps he or she could change some activities around. Don't forget to take a good, hard look at your schedule. Maybe you can get a different work or class schedule. Perhaps you could adjust when you see your own friends. Your child is a central part of your life and it is important that your schedule reflects this.

If you find that because of the way the child's schedule and the other parent's schedule are arranged they are not seeing as much of each other as they should, talk to the other parent. Ask if he or she has noticed this. Perhaps he or she could make some changes to his or her schedule. You can't force him or her to do this, but you can show that it is important to you that your child has enough time with the other parent. Remember that changes to the parenting schedule can only be made if both you and the other parent agree to them.

Equal Time Problems

You have a set schedule you are supposed to follow. Look at your schedule and figure out approximately how many days or hours the schedule gives the other parent with your child in a week or in a month. If changes are made to the schedule, he or she should still end up with roughly the same amount of time. If visitation is normally scheduled from 7 P.M. on Friday to 2 P.M. on Sunday, and an alteration is made so your child doesn't go until 9 P.M. on Friday, then technically, you should change the Sunday time to 4 P.M.

This can get very nit-picky if you or the other parent try to be militant about it. Look to see that the other parent is getting roughly the same amount of time each month. A few hours here or there aren't going to make a huge difference, but if he or she is losing a lot of time on a consistent basis, he or she may become angry about it or feel cheated. Additionally, you need to remember that this time really belongs to your child, so he or she is the one being cheated.

Some Points of Confusion About Schedules

Sometimes talking about schedules can get confusing. If the other parent is supposed to have your child every other weekend, for example, this means that you have the child weekend A, the other parent has the child weekend B and then it is your turn again weekend C and so on.

If you and the other parent agree to swap weekends, things can get confusing. If the normal schedule of weekends is:

> Weekend A: you
> Weekend B: the other parent
> Weekend C: you
> Weekend D: the other parent

and you and the other parent agree that you are going to swap weekends A and B, then the new schedule would be:

> Weekend A: the other parent
> Weekend B: you
> Weekend C: you
> Weekend D: the other parent.

Don't get confused and think that weekend C should be the other parent's since you are on an alternating schedule. You substituted weekend B for weekend A, which was your regularly scheduled weekend. Weekend C is your next regularly scheduled weekend. The same applies if the other parent ends up with two weekends in row because of a change.

Another point of confusion is holidays. If your holiday falls on a weekend or day that is your regularly scheduled time, you will get your holiday and regularly scheduled time simultaneously. If it is your holiday and it falls during the other parent's time, you get the time and the other parent does not. Holidays "trump" regularly scheduled time.

If your holiday falls on a weekend or time the child is normally scheduled to be with the other parent, you will get that holiday and you will also have your next regularly scheduled weekend, even if this means you get two weekends in a row. For example:

> Weekend A: your regular time
> Weekend B: the other parent's regular time, but it is Christmas and it is your turn to have it, so the child will be with you
> Weekend C: your regular time
> Weekend D: the other parent's regular time.

Keep in mind that this can work the other way too—the other parent may end up having the child for two or three weekends some years because a holiday he or she is scheduled to have falls during your regular visitation time.

There can be confusion if your court ordered schedule just says "alternating holidays." You and the other parent need to sit down and work out what these holidays will be. You also want to be sure that you understand if you are alternating the holidays by year, for example:

> Christmas 2003: your turn
> Christmas 2004: the other parent's turn
> Christmas 2005: your turn

Or if you are actually taking an every-other-holiday approach to things, for example:

> Year 2003:
> New Year's Day: your turn
> Easter: the other parent's turn
> Memorial Day: your turn
> Fourth of July: the other parent's turn
> Labor Day: your turn

This continues throughout the year, so that you have one holiday and the other parent gets the next one. This kind of schedule is hard to follow, especially if your family always celebrates on Christmas Eve and the other parent's family always celebrates on Christmas Day—this kind of schedule could have your child missing both family celebrations.

Try to avoid these kinds of scheduling confusions by always writing schedules out on a calendar so you can see them and being clear with the other parent about schedule changes.

Dealing with Schedule Violations

There will be times when both you and the other parent will make mistakes with regard to the schedule. Try to give each other some slack. No one's perfect and mistakes are going to happen. If you find that the other parent consistently makes mistakes about the schedule, first think about what kind of mistakes they are. Do these mistakes actually benefit you? For example, if the parent regularly picks your child up for visitation late, this actually gives you more time. You might not want to complain—but you need to remember that again, your child is the one being cheated. However, this can be inconvenient if you have other things planned or other commitments to meet. If this is the case, or if the mistakes happen all the time, then you need to talk to the other parent. Explain that many mistakes are happening and you'd like to make sure that you both have the same dates or times written down. Suggest to the other parent that these mix-ups are confusing or frustrating or upsetting for your child. Nicely ask if you can all try to stick to the schedule.

If this doesn't work, maybe you could make some permanent changes to the schedule. Perhaps the other parent is consistently late because he or she is getting caught in traffic or is getting out of work late. Changing the time should help eliminate the problem.

You can also try to set some ground rules. For example, if visitation is supposed to start at 9 A.M. on Saturday, tell the other parent that if he or she does not call in advance to make a schedule change and he or she is not there to pick up the child by 10, then the visit will be forfeited. This is a tough approach, but you are not at the other parent's beck and call. You do have a life and cannot always stay at home all day on the chance that he or she might decide to show up several hours late. Be aware that this will be difficult for your child. You will look like the bad guy. Remember that you will be showing your child that we all have rules, schedules and deadlines to follow. Do not say negative things about the other parent in front of the child! Simply explain what the rule is and what has happened. If you find that you have a very difficult relationship with the other parent, you may want to document all of this in a journal or on the calendar, so that you can't be accused of trying to interfere with visitation.

If none of this works, then you are going to have to tell the other parent that the schedule has to be followed and if he or she refuses to, then you will have to call your attorney. Your attorney may be able to talk to the other parent's attorney and convince him or her to follow it or you may have to go to mediation or to court as a last resort. Keep in mind though that nobody can force the other parent to spend time with your child! If he or she doesn't want to show up, there isn't much you can do about it.

11

DEALING WITH OTHER PEOPLE

Divorce or separation is a very personal matter. While going through the process, you probably realized that more people were involved in your personal matter than you ever dreamed possible. Now that you are through the process and are living with your parenting plan, you will find that you are not done with other people's involvement in your relationship with your child.

Schools

It is essential that your child's school know about the divorce or separation. Divorce and separation can affect children's performance and behavior in school and it is important your child's teacher have this information. You will also want to be sure that the school has up-to-date addresses and phone numbers for you and the other parent. If the other parent has the right to access your child's school records (and almost all non-custodial parents have this right), the school will need to be notified of this. You can let the other parent do this or you can do it yourself if you'd like to.

You can contact your child's school and ask that separate parent-teacher conferences be scheduled for you and the other parent. If you are comfortable attending one conference together, you may still do so. Discuss with the other parent whether he or she will attend school events and whether you will sit together.

You do need to remember that contact with your child's teacher is not an opportunity to complain about the other parent, blame things on the other parent, or pump the teacher for information about the other parent. The teacher can offer insight as to how your child is adjusting to the change in home life and how it is impacting school performance. If your child consistently has problems the day after transition between parents, this is an indication that there are some adjustment issues you need to deal with. Take a look at the timing of the visits. Would it be easier for the child if he or she came home a bit earlier? Would the adjustment be better if the other parent took the child to school instead of returning him or her home the night before? Take a look at what changes you can make and try different things so that you can find what works best.

To help make things simpler in your dealings with the school, it may be a good idea to agree on some rules about which parent will be responsible for what. For example, it makes sense that the parent who "has" the child for the day in question be the one to sign a permission slip for a field trip or after school event. For example, if your child is going to be with the other parent from Wednesday night to Saturday morning and the school sends home a permission slip for a field trip that will happen on Friday, it may make sense to let the other parent be the one to sign it. Of course, both parents need to know about it, in case of emergency or in case there is a change in the parenting schedule.

Additionally, children sometimes are required to get a signature from a parent on a test or report card. You can decide that one of you will always be responsible for this or you can decide that whichever parent is with the child when he or she comes home from school with the item will be the one to sign it. Make sure the parent who is not signing has a chance to see the report card or test. Some parents decide that one parent will handle all paperwork for the sport the child plays and the other parent will handle all school paperwork. If you can have a standard plan in place for these kinds of things, you can prevent confusion.

Health Care Workers

You need to contact your child's doctor(s) and dentist to inform them about the divorce or separation. This is particularly important information for a pediatrician to have, because the emotions your child experiences during the post-divorce period can have an impact on his or her health. Be sure the office has up-to-date addresses and phone numbers for both parents. You'll also want to be sure to let them know about any changes in insurance and responsibility for the medical or dental bills. Make sure that you and the other parent both have health insurance cards for your child, so either of you can get medical care for him or her at any time. The other parent may request that the doctor separately inform him or her about your child' health, if he or she was given the right to access your child's medical information. Some parents take turns accompanying children on medical and dental appointments so that both have a chance to speak to the health care professionals. Think about this option and discuss it with the other parent.

If you have sole custody, which means you have the sole authority to make important decisions about your child, this can mean that a doctor or hospital may not allow the other parent to authorize medical care for your child. This can be a real problem if you can't be reached or are out of town. If you feel that you want the other parent to be able to authorize medical care, then it is a good idea to give him or her a written authorization to do so (and have it notarized). Give a copy of this signed and notarized form to the other parent, to your child's pediatrician and dentist (and other doctors your child sees regularly), and to the school. If you and the other parent have joint legal custody, with residence to you and visitation to the other parent, you do not need to create such an authorization, since the other parent has the legal authority to make decisions about your child. You should point this out to your pediatrician and other health care workers, though, to prevent any confusion.

AUTHORIZATION TO OBTAIN MEDICAL CARE

I, _____ am the mother/father of the child _____, whose date of birth is _____. I have sole custody of the child. I hereby authorize _____, the mother/father of the child, to make medical/dental/health decisions about the child and to authorize treatment for the child in my absence or if I cannot be reached.

_____
print your name

_____   _____
sign your name   date

Your Family and Friends

Now that you are divorced or separated, your family and friends are more important than ever to you. Your family and close friends are also an important part of your child's support system. While you want your child to continue to have contact with these people, you need to strike a balance. If you fill the time you spend with your child by always having a friend or relative over to your home, you are sending a message that you do not want to be alone with your child. Involve your child with your family and friendships, but make sure you have time alone to maintain your own relationship.

It is fine to have a friend drop over for a few hours while your child is with you. However, you are using your friends and family as a crutch if you need them with you all the time.

The Other Parent's Family and Friends

Just as it is important for your child to have contact with your family and friends, he or she needs to remain in contact with the other parent's family and friends. You must refrain from making negative or derogatory comments about any of these people. Allow your child to talk about the visits with these people and participate in the conversation, but do not press your child for details or be overly inquisitive. In short, it is none of your business.

If you find that the other parent is always with family or friends during visitation, this is something you might want to calmly discuss alone with him or her. Point out that you don't mind that he or she brings the child along sometimes, but that you want him or her to know that the child also needs alone time. Be aware that some non-custodial parents use other people as a crutch when they don't feel confident enough to be alone with their child. You may need to help the other parent develop some confidence.

Should you run into any of these former relatives or former friends, be polite but distant. Do not get into a discussion about the divorce, separation or about your child. The details of these things are for you and the other parent only. You do not need to justify or explain anything to your former relatives or former friends. Doing so will likely only result in bad feelings or conflict.

Your New Partner

If you have someone new in your life that is important to you, you need to do some evaluating before involving that person with your child. If you are at a point where you are casually dating different people, it is best not to introduce them to your child. It can be confusing. It is OK for you to date and for your child to know that you do. You are supposed to go on living!

If you have one person you are seeing regularly, you need to decide how serious you are about the new relationship. If you think this person is important to you, it is fine to introduce him or her to your child. You should never present the new person as a replacement for the other parent and it is very important that you continue to have time alone with your child. Children and teens will be curious about this relationship and may ask if you plan on remarrying. It's best to be honest, but don't go into the details about your relationship. You should also expect your child to exhibit some resentment, coldness, or rudeness towards this person. This will pass with time.

You will need to make your own personal and moral judgment about a new partner spending the night with you when your child is present. It is never appropriate for a child to witness overt adult sexual behavior. Here are some general tips about dating:

➤ Date if you feel it is something you want to do.
➤ Don't get your child involved with all of the different people you date if you are playing the field.
➤ Be honest with your child about the fact that you are dating.
➤ Expect your child to have mixed emotions about it.
➤ Introduce your child to someone that is special with whom you are having (or hoping to have) a long term relationship.
➤ Decide if you feel sleepovers with dates are appropriate when your child is at your home.
➤ Never make your child feel that a new partner is a replacement for the other parent.
➤ Don't let your dating life fill all of your free time with your child.
➤ Don't expect your child to be thrilled you are dating or to accept a new partner quickly.
➤ Never allow your child to witness inappropriate adult sexual activity.
➤ Don't make your new partner a part of the family too quickly.
➤ Don't discuss your dating life with the other parent or expect him or her to discuss his or hers with you.
➤ Don't get your child involved in your emotional roller coaster. He or she is not a confidant or pal. Keep any romantic angst to yourself.
➤ Remember that while you are supposed to have an adult social life, you want your child to feel cared for and important in your life.

Should you reach the point where you are going to remarry, you need to set some ground rules. The new spouse should never be referred to as "Mom" or "Dad" or whatever name the child uses for the other parent. The new spouse can have authority over the child since they will be sharing the same house, but you as the parent should be the one making all the important decisions about the child. If there are step-siblings, you need for your child to know he or she is not being replaced. The same goes for any half-siblings that are later born into the family. See the resources in Appendix B or C for information and support as you form a step family.

The Other Parent's New Partner

If the other parent is dating, you should not be involved. It may be difficult, you may feel hurt and betrayed, but you have to stay out of it. If your child talks about the other person, it is fine to listen but don't make snide comments, ask questions or get involved in any way. If the other parent begins dating one person seriously you will certainly hear more about it. Don't believe everything your child says. If you run into the person, be civil and polite.

If your child is witnessing inappropriate adult sexual activity at the other parent's home, your first step should be, as always, to talk to the other parent. You can't always believe everything your child is telling you. Express your concerns to the other parent. If you still believe that this is occurring, or your child continues to tell you about other instances, then you need to talk to your attorney if your discussions with the other parent have not improved the situation. Another option you have is to contact your local department of social or human services or state child abuse hotline.

Should the other parent remarry, you can expect your child to be excited, happy, depressed, nervous, left out, angry, jealous and so on. Your child will need reassurance that he or she will always be an important person to both you and the other parent. Remember that no stepparent can ever take your place or fill your shoes. It is not acceptable for the new stepparent to be called by the same name as your child calls you ("Mom," "Daddy," "Ma," "Father," etc.), and if this is happening, you should have a polite and calm conversation with your child's other parent to express how you feel about this. If your child is the one initiating this, tell him or her how important your relationship is. Explain that it hurts your feelings that this is happening. Ultimately the other parent will be the one who will have to resolve this issue since it is happening in his or her home. Adjusting to a new stepparent will take time and you need to be patient with your child while this is happening.

Here are some things to keep in mind when parenting within a step-family:

> ➤ Don't expect your child to be thrilled about your remarriage.
> ➤ Explain to your child that the new spouse is not a replacement for the other parent.
> ➤ Help your child get to know stepsiblings before a marriage.
> ➤ Expect conflict in your stepfamily.
> ➤ Don't ask or allow your child to call the new stepparent by the same name he or she calls the other parent.

➤ Make sure your child knows that he or she is an important part of the new family.

➤ Help the new spouse develop a relationship with your child. Do not expect them to have a parent-child relationship. The relationship cannot immediately take on this form. Eventually your child may come to see the stepparent as a third parent.

➤ Allow the stepparent to have reasonable authority over your child, but make sure everyone in the family remembers that YOU are the child's parent.

➤ Take the time to listen to your child's feelings and thoughts about the new marriage.

➤ Continue to respect your child's visitation schedule and make sure that it is a priority in your family.

➤ If the new spouse has children, try to rearrange scheduling so that all of the children can be together sometimes. They will never develop good relationships if they hardly ever see each other.

➤ Take the time to make your new marriage as successful as possible. Another divorce isn't going to be good for anyone.

➤ Get some support from a stepfamily association or a counselor experienced in stepfamily issues if necessary.

➤ Make sure your child is an involved, active and important member of your new family.

Dealing with Stepfamily Problems

If you or the other parent remarries, your child is going to have to learn to live in a stepfamily. If you both remarry, your child will be in two stepfamilies. Living in a stepfamily can be a balancing act for all involved, particularly if there are stepchildren or half-siblings in the family. If there are problems at the other parent's home, you can let the other parent know if your child is upset, but generally you need to stay out of it—unless you believe your child is emotionally or physically in danger.

If problems develop in your own stepfamily, try to deal with them with patience and understanding. Living in a stepfamily is not easy for children and there can be lots of issues. Join a local stepfamily support group, read some of the books recommended in Appendix B or C or visit some of the websites listed in the appendix. Get some support and don't be afraid to get some help from a counselor who specializes in stepfamily issues. Adjusting to a stepparent can be just as difficult as adjusting to a divorce.

12

SPECIAL SITUATIONS

The goal of this book is to help you manage visitation by pointing out the pitfalls and problems you face as a custodial parent and helping you cope with it all in a way that will allow you to raise a happy and well-adjusted child.

However, there are times when you can't manage the situation on your own and it is important to be able to recognize what these situations are and how to get help. This chapter will help you do that.

Physical or Sexual Abuse

If your child has actually been, or you honestly believe he or she may have been physically or sexually abused by the other parent (or by anyone else for that matter), you must first obtain whatever emergency medical care is needed. Usually this means getting the child to a hospital or doctor immediately. You need to contact your state's social services department or the police to report the abuse. (State abuse hotline numbers are listed in Appendix D.) You then will need to cooperate with the caseworkers who investigate the report. Obtain counseling for your child to assist with the mental and emotional damage that has occurred. Contact your attorney to find out if you should seek sole custody or have visitation supervised.

Substance Abuse

If the other parent has developed a substance abuse problem, you need to consult your attorney about how to deal with the situation. If you have developed a substance abuse problem, it is important that you get help. Talk to your child about your problem, what you are doing about it and how you got into this situation. Encourage him or her to avoid making the same mistakes.

If you suspect or know that your child is using drugs, it is imperative that you get him or her help immediately. There are some organizations and information clearinghouses listed in Appendix B and C that can help you with this. You need to speak with the other parent immediately so you can work together to solve this, if possible. Get a referral to a treatment center or substance abuse counselor from your child's pediatrician. As a last resort, you can contact law enforcement, but this should only be a last resort.

Mental Illness

It is normal for your child to react to the divorce or separation and resulting adjustment with anger, depression, fear, regression (acting younger than the child is), sadness, guilt and so on. For some children, these reactions might be quite severe. There is a fine line between a normal reaction to the divorce and an abnormal reaction. If your child endangers him or herself or threatens to harm him or herself, you need to get mental health assistance immediately. If your child's attitude and emotions seem to make it impossible for him or her to live a normal life, you need to get help. Chapter 2 lists the symptoms of depression. Consult that list if depression is a concern.

You know your child. If you feel that his or her reaction is just not right, get help. It is a good idea to talk to the other parent about this. Working together is the best way to handle this situation. If there is question in your mind at all as to whether your child would benefit from mental health assistance, then you should err on the side of caution and get help. Your child's pediatrician can make a referral to a counselor or therapist. A child who does not need therapy will be identified by the therapist, so you won't do any harm by taking your child to a therapist.

SIGNS YOU MAY NEED TO GET HELP FOR YOUR CHILD

> he or she is extremely detached and displays very little emotion or reaction to anything;
> he or she talks about suicide or harming him or herself or actually attempts self-harm;
> he or she is frequently violent and destructive;
> he or she is withdrawn, sad, and depressed;
> he or she is overly nervous, obsessive, or compulsive;
> he or she cries far more than is normal for the age;
> he or she is constantly hostile to you or the other parent;
> he or she is experiencing serious difficulty at school (and this is a new problem); and/or
> he or she has regressed substantially and has remained so for a long time.

> **NOTE**
> These are some general warning signs. Only a trained mental health worker can know if your child needs treatment. These descriptions are basic and are not determinative. It is normal for a child to display some of these signs (but self-harm is *never* normal) in a mild way when coping with divorce, separation and visitation. You should be concerned if you see these symptoms on a long-term consistent basis. If you are ever in doubt, seek assistance from a mental health worker.

If you feel that you are experiencing depression, anxiety or other mental health problems, seek help. There are many treatments available and it is important to recognize that these are illnesses in the same way that pneumonia or asthma are. Don't worry about what other people think. You can't be an adequate parent if your own problems go untreated.

If the other parent exhibits signs of mental illness, you need to contact your attorney. Family and friends may be able to support your suspicions about this. Do not involve your child! If you feel your child is unsafe at the other parent's home, contact the child abuse hotline for your area and speak to your attorney about temporarily stopping visitation.

Violation of the Terms of Visitation

If the other parent is continuously and grossly late for the pick-up or drop-off and you have tried discussing this with him or her to no avail, you need to talk to your attorney. Keep in mind that the goal should be to set up a schedule that can be followed by both of you. Your goal is not to punish the other parent or attempt to keep him or her away from your child.

If the other parent misses visitation completely on a regular basis, you have tried talking about it calmly and rationally, and it continues to happen, you need to consult your attorney. Again, keep in mind that you do not want to keep him or her away from your child, but instead want to create a schedule that can be followed reliably. Visitation is something that is good for your child, so you should try to work with the other parent to find a schedule that can be followed. Chapter 6 has more information about this.

If the other parent fails to bring your child back from visitation and you are fairly certain this is not just a slight delay, you should first call the other parent and ask if there has been a schedule mix up. If he or she refuses to return your child, or if you cannot locate him or her and you feel that this could be an abduction situation, you need to contact the police and you attorney immediately.

Bad Parenting by the Other Parent

Almost all divorced or separated parents, at some time or another, have reservations about the other parent's parenting abilities. If you're honest with yourself, you've probably had doubts about your own parenting abilities at some point. No one is perfect, after all. Just because you do not agree with the decisions or actions of the other parent does not mean that he or she is an unfit parent. It is helpful to remember that at some point, you did believe he or she was a good parent, otherwise you would not have chosen to have children with him or her.

There are people who are simply terrible parents. If the other parent is part of this group, you need to ask yourself why you did not act on it during the divorce. If nothing has changed between then and now, perhaps you are just feeling very angry, hurt or depressed. If you believed this was true, why didn't you take steps to protect your child then? How serious are the problems?

There are certainly instances in which people have drastically changed after a divorce. Some people even develop mental illnesses after a divorce. If this has happened with the other parent, you should contact your attorney to discuss your options, which may include seeking reduced or supervised visitation. It is also very important that you document everything you can—keep a log or diary of the incidents that have concerned you and obtain copies of all medical or school records that will support your case. DO NOT INVOLVE YOUR CHILD at this stage. If you do return to court or mediation, you will need to tell your child that this is happening and provide a brief explanation, such as, "Mom/Dad and I are having some differences of opinion about where you should spend your time and we are asking the judge to help us."

You may think that the other parent was a terrible parent before the divorce or separation and nothing has changed. You did all you could to let the court know, but feel that you weren't taken seriously or that the visitation that was ordered is simply too much considering the other parent's abilities. You must now keep track of all problems and concerns (in a log or journal) so that you can return to court in the future with more proof and convince the judge to see things your way.

While necessary in some situations, this kind of approach will ensure that your relationship with the other parent continues to be difficult and will impact your child. What is best for your child is for you to avoid conflict with the other parent when possible. Unless you honestly feel your child is in danger, or is extremely miserable when with the other parent, try to just get on with things and accept your situation.

Nonpayment of Child Support

If the other parent is supposed to pay you child support and is consistently late or misses payments, you need to speak to your attorney or to your state child support collection unit. It is very important that both you and the other parent understand that child support is not tied to visitation. IF THE OTHER PARENT DOESN'T PAY CHILD SUPPORT, THIS DOES NOT MEAN YOU CAN DENY HIM OR HER VISITATION. The two things are completely separate.

Sometimes non-custodial parents think that they can reduce child support if they spend more time with the child. For example, if you go out of town for a week and you and the other parent agree that he or she will care for the child in your absence, child support still must be paid for that week, even though the other parent is the one who is caring for the child that entire week.

You should also know that the other parent cannot dictate how you spend child support money. Spending it on the mortgage or on car repairs is perfectly fine; you could even go spend it on a new pair of shoes for yourself if you really wanted to. You do have an obligation to make sure your child is supported and to make sure he or she is cared for adequately, so it only makes sense to try to use child support money to do so.

In general, you need to keep child support issues separate from visitation issues and make sure you do not get your child involved in child support problems. Try not to let child support disputes poison your parenting relationship.

Changing Custody

After living as a residential parent for a while, some parents come to the conclusion that the arrangement is not working. Think about why you feel this way. Is your child consistently unhappy? If so, try some therapy. Are you unhappy? Many divorced parents do experience feelings of unhappiness, but it does go away—by itself or with therapy. Look at what is upsetting you about the situation and try to change things. Moving your child over to live with the other parent may not be the best solution for any of you. If you are feeling like you need more time to yourself, see if the other parent is able to extend visitation times temporarily to see if this helps. Get help from friends and family. Make some lifestyle changes so you are not so stressed out. If none of this is possible, or it doesn't solve the underlying problem, contact your attorney.

Getting your attorney involved will often mean a return to court and this will have an effect on your child. Children are aware of court proceedings simply because it is almost impossible to hide it from them. Also, your child may be assigned a law guardian or guardian ad litem who will represent your child in court. This attorney will need to meet with and speak to your child. It is always best to try to work something out on your own without a return to court. If you and the other parent just can't find a compromise, try using a mediator. Your child needn't be involved in mediation as he or she is in a formal court proceeding.

You Want to End Visitation

Some parents feel overwhelmed and frustrated with the demands of a parenting plan. They are tired of dealing with the other parent, tired of trading the child back and forth, and just want visitation to disappear. They decide that they never want to see the other parent, they never want to speak to him or her again, and want there to be no more visitation.

Your child needs to have a second parent in his or her life. Make some changes to make things easier on yourself. Ask that the other parent not come in the house when picking up or dropping off the child. Simply refuse to argue with him or her. Agree to speak with him or her only when someone else you trust is present. If you must, have all schedule changes or negotiations handled by your attorney. Do whatever you have to do to ensure that your child will have two parents while reducing the stress you are under.

Consider all the possibilities of what is really bothering you. Are you not getting enough sleep? Is your schedule too crowded? Are you worried about money? Are you having too many conflicts with the other parent? Are you and your child having conflicts? Try to get at the root of the problem and see if you can fix that first. If you don't see what you can change, try seeing a therapist. He or she may be able to help you change things to make them easier to cope with. You have to realize that the other parent is not going to change, and since visitation is a basic fact of life now, you have to find some way to deal with it. Whatever you do, don't give up. When you created this child, you gave an unbreakable lifetime commitment to always do your best to love and care for him or her, and this includes making sure your child has a second parent.

Supervised Visitation

Some non-custodial parents are only permitted to have supervised visitation with their children. This means that another adult, who is approved by the court, must be present during parenting time. If the other parent has supervised visitation, you probably had a good reason for requesting it or the judge had a good reason for ordering it.

In most cases, supervised visitation does not go on forever and if the other parent proves that he or she can handle visitation, the visits become unsupervised. The goal really is to help the other parent reach a point where he or she can have normal access to the child. Many non-custodial parents are required to attend parenting classes, support groups, or therapy to help prepare them for this.

A child who goes to supervised visitation may be confused and not understand why he or she cannot see the other parent anywhere else. Explain to your child that this is where he or she will be seeing Mom/Dad at least for a while because that is how the judge decided visitation is to happen. Don't make yourself out as the bad guy here by explaining that it was what you wanted, too. You need to encourage your child to go to visitation and have a good time with the other parent. You should not quiz him or her about how the visits went. Contact the person who is supervising visitation if you want a report.

If you have a problem with the person who is supervising the visitation or the location it is taking place at, try to come up with some alternatives and contact your attorney about them.

If the other parent has a history of violence or instability, it can be difficult to take your child to supervised visitation. It is important that you reassure yourself that your child will be safe. If visitation is at a facility, familiarize yourself with it first. Talk to the person who will be supervising and get a sense for how carefully things are monitored and what kinds of activities will happen. Once you have done this, you simply have to let go and allow your child to go. Stay in touch with the supervisor and your attorney, so you can monitor the situation.

Homosexuality

Sometimes a marriage or relationship ends because one of the partners realizes he or she is homosexual. Other times a discovery such as this happens or comes to light after the divorce or separation. If you are the parent who has made this discovery, it is your choice as to how open you would like to be about it with your child. Certainly your child's age should play an important part in how much you choose to discuss. It is wise to make sure the other parent is aware of your situation first, and it is also a good idea to let him or her know you are going to discuss it with the child so he or she is not blindsided. In introducing your child to same sex dates and partners, you should follow the same guidelines included in Chapter 11 for dating.

If the other parent is homosexual, you need to deal with your own feelings about the revelation. It is important that you not make any negative or derogatory remarks to your child about this. Also, it should be up to the other parent if he or she would like to let the child know about his or her sexual orientation. Your role will be to support the child and provide support after the information is shared. It is important that you understand that courts do not believe that a person's sexual orientation affects his or her parenting abilities.

Teens

If you are the parent of a teen, you know that everything is different for teens. You probably had to modify your house rules, your discipline style and even your communication style when your child became a teen. Teens handle divorce differently from children of any other age. While they do experience the same feelings of loss, grief, anger, sadness, etc., they also take blame on themselves for the divorce. Many also see the divorce as proof that they will never have a stable relationship and that they should never get married. You will need to work through these feelings with your teen and help him or her realize that no one is to blame for the divorce and that it is no prediction of the child's future relationships.

Teens need to be consulted about parenting plans and schedules. They are at a point in their lives where their friends are the most important thing in the world and they are also working very hard to be independent of their parents. While teens should have input, they should not be permitted to make the final decisions.

As you begin to implement your parenting plan involving your teen, you will meet with resistance, outbursts and even refusals to communicate. Your parenting plan is flexible, but it is not optional. Allowances can be made for your teen's schedule, job and friends, but the bottom line is that the plan must be basically honored. More information about teens is contained in Chapter 13.

Children Who Refuse Visitation

Children of all ages sometimes will refuse to go with the other parent for visitation. Your position must be that the schedule is flexible, but it is not optional. You can and will make changes, but the basic schedule itself must be implemented.

What do you do if an eight-year-old refuses to go out the door? What if a five-year-old hides under his bed? First, assess what the problem is. Does the child resist the transition, but adjust once it is over? If so, think of ways you can ease the transition. See Chapter 8 for ideas about easing transition problems.

If nothing works, and your child still refuses to go, you must insist that he or she go. As a parent, you are often in the position of making your child do something he or she does not wish to do. It's never fun and it's never pretty, but as a parent you must enforce your authority. Your child may be unconsciously testing you to see how serious you are about your commitment to visitation. It's important that you and the other parent present a united front about this issue. Discuss it with the other parent to make sure you are both on the same page with this.

Parents Who Refuse to Exercise Visitation

Sometimes parents arrive late or forget about visitation. This is normal. Talk with the other parent about your concerns. Other times, parents simply do not show up for visitation time and time again. If this happens, try directly asking the other parent why this is happening. You should keep a record of these occurrences. You do not have to cover up for the other parent or try to make excuses for his or her absence. It is OK to tell your child you don't know why he or she did not come, but it is not OK for you to fly off the handle in front of your child.

If your child's other parent consistently and regularly is skipping visitation without calling or rescheduling, you need to consult your attorney. You are also going to need to get your child some help from a therapist or counselor. Being abandoned by a parent is traumatic and you need to make sure your child has the support necessary to cope with this situation.

It is OK to be honest with your child about what is happening. Explain that the other parent, for some reason, is missing visitation. Help your child understand that it is not his or her fault and that the parent must have some problems he or she needs to work through. Explain that it is OK to feel hurt or angry and help your child see that the other parent truly is to be pitied for missing out on visitation. Continue to try to encourage the other parent to exercise the same visitation.

Things That Supercede Visitation

There are situations that will essentially supercede your schedule:

> ➢ a seriously ill or hospitalized child;
> ➢ extreme weather conditions that prevent travel;
> ➢ family emergencies,
> ➢ a parent's serious illness; or,
> ➢ death of a family member.

If your child is quite ill, you should try to arrange for the other parent to see him or her, but this shouldn't be done according to the schedule. Short daily visits work best. If the child is in the hospital, you can take turns visiting at different parts of the day.

If there is a weather emergency that makes it unsafe to travel, the child should stay where he or she is. You can resume your normal schedule after it is over. The child should have phone contact (if possible) with the other parent.

If either you or the other parent is seriously ill, you will be unable to care for your child. The healthy parent can step in and help can also be found from relatives and friends.

Should a family member pass away, your child, if he or she is old enough, will want to be able to be with that side of the family and attend gatherings and services. Make adjustments to the schedule to allow for this.

Other unexpected situations can arise, such as a parent being delayed by a car accident or an emergency at work. You and the other parent should try to be flexible in these situations. The important thing is to make sure your child is not frightened by the unexpected change or delay.

Relocation

There may come a point in your life where you find you need or want to move to another area. The first thing you need to do is consult your attorney. There are limits on your ability to do so. Often a custody agreement or judgment will contain specific restrictions about the custodial parent's ability to relocate. The law in many states limits your right to relocation if you are the custodial parent and requires court permission, or agreement by the non-custodial parent.

If you are not able to get clearance to move, you will need to carefully weigh your choices. You can stay where you are and find some way to make it work or you might find that you have no choice but to leave. If you are not permitted to take your child with you, then you may find yourself trading places with the other parent—with you becoming the non-custodial parent. If this is the case, you need to flip this book over and read the other side. Remember that there is nothing wrong with being the non-custodial parent and that you can continue to have an excellent relationship with your child no matter how far apart you live.

Special Needs Children

If you have a special needs child, you are probably a bit apprehensive about visitation. Make sure that your spouse is educated about the child's needs, medications, emergency care, etc. It is a good idea to write all of this information down and make sure it travels with the child. You might also suggest that the other parent talk with the child's doctor or therapist to fully understand the child's limitations and necessary care. Make sure that the child's medications travel with him or her.

Special needs are not an excuse to limit visitation. These children need both parents just as much as other children do.

Parental Abduction

Parental abduction accounts for the majority of missing children. Should this ever happen in your family, you need to immediately contact the police with a recent photo of your child and spouse if possible. You need to obtain a copy of your judgment or order that gives you custody and provide this to the police.

One way to prevent abduction out of the country is to apply for a passport for your child and keep it in a safety deposit box. Only one passport per person can be issued. Local police often sponsor child safety days where they will photograph and fingerprint children. If you are truly concerned that abduction is a real possibility, then you must notify your child's school, caregivers, and relatives that they do not have permission to release your child to the other parent. Appendix B and C contain lists of organizations that can assist you should this ever happen.

A Sick Child

If your child is ill when visitation is planned, you should carefully consider your options. If the child has a high fever or has a gastro-intestinal illness, it is probably best if you reschedule because no one wants to be shuffled from house to house in that condition. If you must leave town or for some reason and cannot care for the child, talk to the other parent about him or her coming to stay with the child at your home. If this will not work, the other parent will need to take the child with him or her and make the child as comfortable as possible.

A child with a minor illness, such as a cold, is able to be cared for by the other parent and is able to go as planned. Pack medication and anything else that will keep your child comfortable. Do what you can to make sure your child will be cared for properly and then let it go. Most non-custodial parents are capable of caring for a sick child.

Military Personnel/Travel for Work

If the other parent is in the military or travels for work, he or she may be away for long periods of time. Read the section about long distance parenting to help your child cope with this. When the other parent is in the area, your child will want to spend time with him or her. It's important that you remain flexible and encourage visitation when it is possible.

If you are a member of the military or travel for your job, you need to make child care arrangements for when you are away. Consider using the other parent as the caregiver. If you use another caregiver, make sure he or she is clear about the visitation schedule. To stay close to your child when you are away, review the tips in the chapter on long distance parenting in the non-custodial parent half of this book.

Imprisonment

Should the other parent be imprisoned, this is sure to be a very difficult situation for your child. You will probably be angry, resentful and disgusted by this situation and your first instinct will be to completely shield your child from this. However, you can't hide the fact that the other parent is in prison. If you don't explain where he or she is, your child will think the other parent has just disappeared and lost interest in him or her. Explain to your child in an age appropriate way where the other parent is and why. It is ok to say that he or she did something wrong or broke a law, since this is the fact of the matter. Answer your child's questions.

Whether your child will visit the other parent will depend in part on where the prison is located. If it is located nearby, an in-person visit can be arranged. The thought of taking your child to a prison may horrify you, but it is important that he or she continue to have contact with the other parent. Your child needs to see that the other parent exists, still loves him or her and is sorry for making the bad decision that led to the prison sentence. This really can be a good experience for your child and can really emphasize the importance of making good decisions.

Many prisons have special children's visitation programs. Call the prison and ask about this or check some of the resources in Appendix B and C. Some of these programs arrange for visitation in a somewhat non-threatening and child-friendly area. If you do take your child for a prison visit, you do need to prepare him or her what for will happen and what will be seen. Try to explain how a prison works and that there are guards and other inmates. Even teens need some preparation before visiting a prison. They may have to go through a metal detector and remove their shoes before being allowed entry. If you show fear or apprehension about the visit, your child will as well. If you can remain calm and matter of fact about, you child is likely to handle it well.

If you are completely opposed to taking your child to the prison, be aware that the other parent may decide to request a court order forcing you to bring the child for visitation. You need to speak to your attorney should this happen. If you live too far away or if you decide not to bring the child to the prison, he or she may maintain contact with the other parent by mail.

If Your Child is Adopted

If your child was adopted (either by both of you or was the natural child of one of you and adopted by the other parent), you should follow the advice offered in this book. Simply because one or both of you is not the child's biological parent should not alter or change anything. When the child was adopted, he or she legally became your child, with both of you as his or her parents. A divorce, separation or end of relationship cannot change that. An adoption cannot be "undone".

If your child knows that he or she was adopted (as most children do these days), he or she may feel as if the divorce or separation means that somehow the adoption will come "undone" as well. Make sure that you reassure him or that this cannot happen and that both of you will continue to be parents in his or her life forever. For some teens, a divorce or separation can spur him or her to try to locate his or her biological parents. Should this issue come up, you should discuss it with your child and offer him or her support, whatever he or she decides to do. It is important to remember that if the biological parents are located, they cannot take your place in your child's life.

Grandparent Visitation

Grandparent visitation has received some publicity in recent years. Many times when there is a divorce or separation, the non-custodial parent's parents make noise about requesting grandparent visitation. The fact is that it is very difficult to get a court to order grandparent visitation. However, just because it is unlikely a court will order you to provide grandparent visitation, does not mean you shouldn't agree to it.

Grandparents are an important part of a child's life and to deny time to the grandparents is really to deprive your child of this important relationship. It's likely that you and your former in-laws harbor unpleasant feelings towards each other. Remember though that this should be about your child and not about your disagreements with your former relatives. You probably feel you don't have enough time with your child and to give up one weekend a month to people you dislike is a terrible imposition. Maybe the grandparents could babysit for you or take your child to some of his or her sports or activities. Think creatively about this. You don't have to agree to ship your child off once a month. Find a way to make the grandparents a part of the child's life.

You may also feel that since they are the other parent's parents, the other parent ought to be the one responsible for making sure the grandparents see the child. To an extent, this is true. If the other parent has a reasonable amount of visitation, there is no reason why he or she can't make sure that the child and grandparents have time together. Discuss this with the other parent. If the other parent lives far away or fails to exercise his or her visitation, you will find that the responsibility for maintaining this relationship will fall on your shoulders.

13

CHILDREN'S AGES AND STAGES

Your child is constantly growing and changing, so it is unrealistic to expect that a visitation plan can be set in stone throughout his or her life. The plan is going to need to change as he or she does. You can make changes simply by talking to the other parent and agreeing on them, you can meet with a mediator who will help you reach an agreement, you can speak to your attorneys and have them reach a settlement or return to court and have the judge decide for you. It's always important to consider your child's current needs when making changes to your schedule.

This chapter will talk about the different needs children have as they grow and will give you some ideas as to how to modify your plan as they do so. Come back to this chapter for help as your child grows or when you or your child start to feel as if the visitation plan needs some changes.

Infants
If you have an infant, your visitation plan may allow the other parent to have frequent short visits or a traditional kind of schedule where he or she has the child for weekends. Generally, short frequent visits work best for infants, so if you have a traditional plan and you find the baby is having difficulty with it, try switching to the other type of plan. Infants may display more frequent crying and problems with eating and digestion when they are disturbed.

One complication to visitation with an infant is breastfeeding. If you are the mother and are breastfeeding, then it will be difficult for the other parent to spend time greater than an hour or two alone with the child. Consider pumping and freezing some breast milk so the other parent can feed the baby from a bottle and thus be able to take the child to his or her home or relative's homes or allow the parent time alone with your child in your home, so you can nurse when needed.

Be aware that breastfeeding can be a very emotional issue. Don't assume that because the other parent wants to be able to spend time alone with your child that he is trying to interfere with it. Explain to the other parent that pediatricians do recommend that children be breastfed for at least one year and discuss the benefits of it with him. Suggest that he talk to the pediatrician to understand it better. Specifically tell him not to give the baby formula and explain how this can complicate breastfeeding. Some mothers are unable to pump milk and feel it is OK for the father to give the baby formula when they are not available for feedings. Talk to your pediatrician or lactation consultant about this before trying it.

If you are the father, and the mother wants to try to continue breastfeeding during visitation times, you should both speak to a lactation consultant about this since it can be difficult, but not impossible.

Sleep issues are always a problem with an infant. You and the other parent need to try to work together to develop a plan. Are you going to try to get the child on a schedule at night and for naps or are you going to let the child decide when sleeping happens? It's important to be consistent and work cooperatively on this. If you are trying to get the child to follow a specific schedule and the other parent doesn't do the same thing, you're going to have a cranky child.

You and the other parent need to work together when solid foods are introduced and need to follow a schedule for your child's meals. Follow a set schedule for introducing new foods—you want to introduce one new food at a time so that if there are any food allergies they can be easily identified. Talk to you pediatrician for more details about this.

Suggest that the other parent get some basic baby equipment to keep at his or her home so everything does not need to be transported each time. He or she can purchase a portable crib instead of a full-size one and a portable highchair seat that straps onto a chair instead of a large free standing highchair.

It is easy when you are the custodial parent of an infant to feel as if you are doing all the hard work and the other parent is showing up for play time. Don't worry, this is only temporary. Some custodial parents feel that they have a hard time getting the non-custodial parent to understand the basics of baby care. Suggest that the other parent come along for well baby visits and encourage discussions with the doctor that will help bring home the points you are having a hard time getting across. Share baby care books with the other parent.

Toddlers

Toddlers are going through many changes and it is best to try to stick to a really tight schedule for visitation. Don't monkey around with it a lot if you can help it.

Toddlers will experience separation anxiety and have trouble separating from whichever parent he or she is with. Deal with separation anxiety by taking a little more time with transitions and making them more gradual. Toddlers also start to display aggression by biting, throwing or hitting. Deal with this by consistently saying no and removing the child from the situation or item.

When your child is a toddler, he or she may be ready to begin spending the night at the other parent's home. Usually one night a week is good way to start, so that they don't go two weeks between sleepovers. You want to get him or her used to this new event and grow accustomed to sleeping at the other parent's home. You also need to adjust to this. This a reality. Your child is going to spend some of his or her time alone with the other parent and will be sleeping there. It is hard to let go, but you have to help your child adjust to this. Toddlers may experience sleep disturbances, especially if they are adjusting to sleeping overnight at the other parent's home for the first time. Talk to the other parent about what works to comfort the child in the night.

Talk with the other parent about things like potty training, discipline and sleeping schedules. Consistency really is important. Share books about what to expect from toddlers with the other parent. Remember that toddlers are all about pushing the limits and your child will want to find out what limits you and the other parent have.

Make sure the other parent has his or her home childproofed so your child cannot reach dangerous things or find small objects to put in his or her mouth.

Tantrums are going to be a fact of life and you and the other parent simply need to learn how to cope with them. A tantrum does not mean you should change your visitation plan. Tantrums are a normal part of your child's development and you both need to develop the skills needed to manage them. Toddlers are difficult even when their parents aren't divorced or separated.

Preschoolers

When your child reaches the preschool age, you'll probably find that he or she is becoming more verbal and cognitive. He or she will probably ask you questions that go to the very root of things, like, "Why do you live here and Dad lives at another house?" Give brief and honest answers to these kinds of questions. A good answer is, "Because some moms and dads don't live together."

Preschoolers can begin to handle a typical visitation schedule, such as every other weekend at the other parent's home. If you do change to this kind of schedule, do so gradually and try to make sure the other parent does continue to have some kind of weekly in-person contact with your child. This is why many parents see their children one week-night each week. Try to make sure your child has phone contact with the other parent on a regular basis as well.

Elementary Children

When your child begins school, you may need to make some adjustments to your schedule. It's important to make sure your child gets enough sleep on school nights. Your child can begin to spend the majority of visitation time on weekends now. Regular in-person contact during the week is important though, so consider working out a schedule where the other parent and child have dinner one weekday evening each week. Keep in contact with the other parent and your child's teacher about how things are going and be prepared to make changes if it seems that the schedule is impacting the child's school behavior. Finding the right schedule can take some trial and error.

Your elementary age child will ask you even more probing questions about the divorce or separation and the reasons for it. Answer questions honestly, but do not give detail or deeply personal information unless it truly is helpful and will not cause the child to see the other parent in a bad light. Children of this age often display their emotions about their family through physical symptoms like headaches and stomachaches. Try to keep your child comfortable and always see a doctor if you believe he or she is truly ill. Be supportive and loving, yet firm about the schedule.

Homework is an important consideration at this age. Elementary students now have more homework than you ever used to at that age. Make sure that your child has time to get homework done at both homes and that the homework gets to school. This requires organization. Encourage your child to ask the other parent for homework help.

Suggest that the other parent help out with a school project. This may mean that they will need some extra time together for trips to the library or to buy materials at a craft store to complete the project on time. Keeping the other parent involved with your child's life will directly benefit your child.

Elementary children also have after school activities and sports to consider. Chapter 13 talks about how to work around these.

Friends are becoming important at this age as well. Your child may wish to spend time with friends during visitation time. You will have to leave this decision to the other parent, but you can suggest that having a friend over will help the child feel at home at the other parent's residence.

Encourage the other parent to attend your child's sports events, concerts and performances. These do not have to fall onto a regularly scheduled visitation day for him or her to attend.

Pre-Teens

Kids in the eight to twelve year age range are often called "tweens" since they are in a stage between early childhood and the teen years. Tweens act a lot like teens sometimes. They are interested in popular culture, fashion, music, movies and trends, but they are still children in many ways. Just because your tween listens to the hottest new music and is sporting a new hairstyle does not mean that he or she doesn't want or need love, attention and time from both parents.

Tweens sometimes try very hard to be perfect in the hopes that this will bring their parents back together. Make sure your child knows no one is perfect and that nothing can bring you and the other parent back together. They also often begin to take sides or assign blame for the divorce or separation (to the parents or themselves). Explain to your child that he or she is not to blame and that there are two people in a marriage or relationship and both in some way cause a break up.

Your child will have even more homework now, lots of friends and activities. It's important that you continue to follow a schedule and make sure that time for both parents is built into the child's life. Let your child be active and busy, find a way for you both to be involved in his or her interests and make sure your child continues to have time to spend together with each parent.

Teens

You remember being a teenager. Nothing about it was easy. It's even harder today, especially when you have parents who live in separate houses and who make different and sometimes competing demands on you.

Your teen deals with the divorce or separation in a way different from younger children. He or she does continue to have feelings of loss, grief, anger and sadness, but also blames him or herself for the situation. Teens frequently feel that they themselves will never be able to have a stable relationship and should avoid marriage. It's important to talk about these feelings with your child and help him or her understand that no blame falls on his or her shoulders and that many marriages do work out.

Teens often feel they have had to grow up too quickly because of the divorce or separation. There isn't much you can do about this, other than to insulate him or her from disputes between you and the other parent and avoid confiding in him or her like a friend. Teens also often worry about money and feel involved with child support and even alimony. Don't involve your teen in child support or alimony matters. Teens do need to start to understand finances and to understand budgets, but you should not unload your financial worries on your teen. Additionally, teens feel a need to take on adult responsibility, to fill the gaps at both homes. Remember, your teen is not an adult and is not a substitute for the other parent and should not be expected to fill his or her role.

Your teen will need to be consulted about the schedule. Independence is so important at this age. Teens not only have a lot of homework and after school activities, but friends are now the most important thing in the world. Many teens also have jobs. Working out a schedule may be difficult. It's going to require some compromise on all fronts. Your teen is working hard at becoming an adult and he or she must learn that compromise is an important skill.

Dating can be a conflict with visitation. What teen is going to give up a date with the guy or girl of his or her dreams to hang out with Mom or Dad? You've got to somehow reach a balance though. If your teen spends every weekend day and evening dating, he or she will never see the other parent and will rarely see you. Perhaps your teen can reserve maybe one weekend a month or two Sundays a month to spend with the other parent. Suggest something similar for your time together as well. Your teen needs to know that you both support his or her lifestyle, but also that you both want to spend time with him or her.

Expect to be met with resistance, outbursts, attitudes, refusals to communicate—all those things you may have done to your parents. You will need to make changes in the schedule to accommodate your teen's life, but there does need to be some kind of regular time for the other parent. Many parents find that they are comfortable without a schedule. They let their teen drop in or stay the night at the other parent's home whenever the mood strikes. If this works for you and the other parent, then go ahead and do it. Other parents feel that they need to have a schedule to follow so they can organize their own lives. You'll have to work out what works best for your family.

If you have a plan that your teen refuses to follow no matter what you do, you need to take a look at it and determine what the problem is. Does he or she resent being away from friends? Can you make any changes or allowances that will make the plan easier to live with? Do you need to make some scheduling changes? Involve your teen in this process and demonstrate that you are willing to be flexible while still maintaining your strong commitment to your relationship.

Unfortunately, there are teens who decide they do not want to go on visitation and do not want to spend time with one of their parents. Period. You must continue to encourage your teen to go on visitation, but when it comes right down to it, you won't be able to force him or her to go. Courts do pay attention to what teens say they want when it comes to visitation.

Talk to the other parent about the situation. Suggest that you both back off and give the teen some space. Skip some planned visits. Emphasize that the other parent should not give up and walk away. Taking some breathing room may be just what is needed, but the other parent shouldn't throw up his or her hands and say "forget it." Your child needs the other parent to care and needs him or her to keep trying. Your teen is exercising his or her independence and you've all got to find a way to work with it.

Adult Children

Once your child is over age 18, he or she is not subject to the visitation plan any longer. This doesn't mean that your work is done! He or she still needs contact with both parents. Just because your child is technically an adult, you should not suddenly unload "the truth" about the other parent. Your child still needs a relationship with the other parent and you still need to keep your mouth shut and your nose out of it. College kids and young adults still need parents.

It is hard to learn to let go and let your child become so independent and watch him or her do things that you see as mistakes. You and the other parent did the best job you could, and your child really will be fine. Pat yourself on the back for creating and raising such a good person.

Siblings

This book has talked about "your child" in a singular sense. Most parents have more than one child. When you have two or more children, you will have to cope with their conflicting schedules, conflicting abilities and, of course, with their conflicts, period.

You'll want to try to keep to a schedule that will allow your children to see the other parent at the same time when possible. They are a family unit and need to spend time all together. Things are going to come up, however. Your daughter might have a basketball game one weekend and your son might have play rehearsal another. Follow the visitation schedule and have the other parent take your kids to their planned events. The other parent can have together time and individual time with your children just as you do.

Brothers and sisters fight. This is just a rule of the universe. Your kids don't fight because you got divorced or separated. They just fight, because that's what siblings do. Set limits, create rules and always make sure no one is physically harmed. Read some parenting books about coping with siblings and share them with the other parent. Discuss possible solutions with the other parent. Since you spend more time with your children, you probably have some strategies for managing them that you can share with the other parent. Remember that the other parent has to be allowed to work things out in his or her own way and you can't dictate how he or she will parent.

There will be a time when your children are certain you or the other parent are playing favorites. Often kids have difficulty understanding that brothers or sisters of different ages need different care, supervision and interaction. Parent as you see fit and reassure them that you both love each child equally but in a unique way.

Talking with the other parent will allow you to coordinate efforts, share insights and work together with regard to your children.

14

CONCLUSION

Now that you've read this book, you know that there is no easy answer or quick fix to make living with visitation easy and comfortable for everyone. Your job as a custodial parent is difficult, and the other parent has a row to hoe that's pretty tough too. You have lots of problems between the two of you that can never be worked out and lots of emotions that pop up at the most inconvenient times, but you are—and always will be—parents together. Your child is your common bond and this book was designed to help you use that to make visitation workable.

Many families get tripped up by problems with visitation and end up constantly going back to court. That kind of life isn't good for anyone. This book has shown you the common pitfalls and ways to work around them and avoid them completely. Now that you've read the book, share it with the other parent. Sit down together and try to follow some of the suggestions in the book. Keep this book on your bookcase and refer back to it as problems and situations come up in the coming years.

Making sure that your child has time with and a decent relationship with the other parent may not be what you really want if you are honest with yourself, but you probably realize by now that it is what your child really and truly needs. It often feels like an imposition; you get tired of trying to accommodate the other parent and sometimes you just wish it would all go away. Hopefully this book has given you some coping strategies to help you get through those days and tips for making things better.

If you come away with nothing else, remember that visitation is not about you or the other parent, but about your child and his or her needs. Making it work sometimes means gritting your teeth, compromising and even sometimes just plain giving in. It will be worth it and your child will benefit from having two parents who work hard to make his or her life better.

Your situation will get easier as you live and work with it and you will see your child adjust as well. The future is bright for both of you and visitation is an important part of that future.

Appendix A

SAMPLE PARENTING PLANS

SAMPLE 1

The following is an informal list of visitation rules developed by one couple:

- ➤ If you will be more than 20 minutes late picking up or dropping off, call and let the other parent know.
- ➤ Discussions about schedule changes are OK in front of the child, but arguments and heated discussions will be postponed until the child is not present.
- ➤ All of the child's laundry will be done at the custodial parent's home.
- ➤ Schedule changes can be made at any time as long as we both agree. Each will notify the other parent as far in advance as possible of any changes.
- ➤ The child can call the parent he or she is away from at any time.
- ➤ The custodial parent will share all school notices, report cards etc with the non-custodial parent.
- ➤ We will attend the same parent-teacher conferences if they can be scheduled conveniently.
- ➤ School books, instruments and sports equipment will travel with the child.
- ➤ We will try to use each other for babysitting if possible.
- ➤ We will try to spend some time together as a family on Christmas Day and will alternate all other holidays.
- ➤ We will respect each other's judgment about bedtimes, curfews and daily schedules.

SAMPLE 2

The following is a formal parenting plan developed by a couple:

We agree that our son, Trevor, shall reside with his mother, Kristin, and spend time with his father, Marcus. Marcus shall have time with Trevor as follows:

a) Every second weekend of the month from school dismissal on Friday until school begins on Monday morning.

b) Every fourth weekend of the month on Saturday from 9 A.M. until 8 P.M.

c) Every Wednesday from school dismissal until 7 P.M.

d) In even numbered years on the following holidays from 10 A.M. until 9 P.M.: New Year's Day, Memorial Day, Labor Day, Thanksgiving, Christmas Eve, the child's birthday.

e) In odd numbered years on the following holidays from 10 A.M. until 9 P.M.: Easter, Fourth of July, Columbus Day, the day after Thanksgiving, Christmas Day, New Year's Eve.

f) 4 days during winter school break and 4 days during spring school break commencing at 10 A.M. on the first day and ending at 8 P.M. on the last day.

g) Every Father's Day and every year on Marcus's birthday.

h) If visitation is supposed to occur on Mother's Day or Kristin's birthday, that day in the schedule will be cancelled.

i) Two full weeks during summer vacation, which will not be scheduled to conflict with Kristin's family's reunion.

j) At other times as we both agree.

k) We will make the schedule together each year in January and adjust it as necessary if we both agree.

We agree that the following procedures will be followed:

1) Kristin shall be responsible for transporting Trevor to Marcus's home at the start of visitation, unless Marcus is scheduled to pick Trevor up at school that day.

2) Marcus shall be responsible for transporting Trevor to Kristin's home at the end of visitation, unless he is scheduled to return him directly to school.

3) Neither parent shall enter the other parent's home unless asked in.

4) Drop off times will have a ten minute leeway in either direction.

5) Trevor will bring clothing for the time he is with Marcus and all clothing that is taken on visitation will be returned with Trevor.

6) All of Trevor's belongings that are taken on visitation will return with him.

7) Trevor will have access to the phone to call or answer a call from whichever parent he is away from at the time.

8) Changes to the visitation schedule must be requested at least 24 hours in advance except in emergency situations.

9) Neither parent will drive Trevor in the car after consuming alcohol.

10) Trevor will not be taken to any bars during visitation.

11) If either parent takes Trevor on vacation, contact information will be given to the other parent.

The following rules will apply to Trevor's routine at both homes:

1) Bedtime is at 9 P.M. unless a special event or special occasion occurs.

2) Both parents will make sure Trevor is dressed appropriately before leaving the house.

3) Computer time is not to occur until after all homework is completed and is limited to one hour per day.

4) Whichever parent is with Trevor at the time is expected to transport him to soccer practice and games.

Marcus has access to Trevor's school and medical records. The following rules will be followed:

1) Marcus is responsible for contacting the school and doctors to get copies of records, report cards, notices and calendars.

2) Marcus will schedule a separate parent-teacher conference if he wishes to attend one.

3) Marcus and Kristin may attend the same school events, concerts, sports games and ceremonies if their schedules allow.

Appendix B

RESOURCES

BOOKS FOR PARENTS

Be a Great Divorced Dad
by Kenneth Condrell

Blending Families: A Guide for Parents, Stepparents and Everyone Building a Successful New Family
by Elaine Fantle Shomberg

Caring for Your Baby and Young Child
by Stephen Shelov, et al

Complete Divorce Recovery Book
by John P. Splinter

The Courage to be a Single Mother: Becoming Whole Again After Divorce
by Sheila Ellison

Co-Parenting After Divorce: How to Raise Happy Healthy Children in Two Home Families
by Diana Shulman

Crazy Time: Surviving Divorce and Building a New Life
by Abigail Trafford

Divorce Casualties: Protecting Your Children From Parental Alienation
by Douglas Darnall

Divorced Dad's Survival Book: How to Stay Connected with Your Kids by David Knox

Families Apart: Ten Keys to Successful Co-Parenting
by Melinda Blau

The Good Divorce: Keeping Your Family Together When Your Marriage Comes Apart
by Constance Ahrons

The Good Housekeeping Book of Child Care: Including Parenting Advice, Health Care, and Child Development for Newborns to Preteens
by Good Housekeeping

"He Hit Me First..." When Brothers and Sisters Fight
by Louise Bates Ames

Helping Children Cope With Divorce
by Edward Teyber

I'm on Your Side: Resolving Conflict with Your Teenage Son or Daughter
by Jane Nelson and Lynn Lott

Joint Custody and Shared Parenting
by Jay Folberg

Live-Away Dads
by William C. Klattle

Mom's House, Dad's House: Making Two Homes for Your Child
by Isolina Ricci

Parenting Teenagers: Systematic Training for Effective Parenting of Teens
by Don Dinkmeyer, et al

Single Fatherhood: The Complete Guide
by Chuck Gregg

Single Mamahood: Advice and Wisdom for the African-American Single Mother
by Kelly WIlliams

The Single Parent Resource
by Brook Noel, ARthur C. Klein, Art Klein

Stepfamily Realities: How to Overcome Difficulties and Have a Happy Family
by Margaret Newman

Still a Dad: The Divorced Father's Journey
by Serge Prengel

Surviving the Breakup: How Children and Parents Cope With Divorce
by Judith S. Wallerstein

The Tween Years
by Donna G. Corwin

The Unexpected Legacy of Divorce: A 25 Year Landmark Study
by Judith Wallerstein

Vicki Lansky's Divorce Book for Parents: Helping Your Child Cope With Divorce and Its Aftermath
by Vicki Lansky

Wonderful Ways to Be a Stepparent
by Judy Ford and Anna Chase

Your Baby and Child
by Penelope Leach

MAGAZINES FOR PARENTS

Dadmag newsletter
http://www.dadmag.com

Divorce Magazine
145 Front Street East, Suite 301
Toronto, Canada M5A-1E3
416-368-8853
http://www.divorcemagazine.com

Fathering Magazine
www.Fathermag.com

Parenting for One Magazine
http://www.parentingforone.com

Single-Parent Family Online Magazine
www.family.org/spfmag/parenting/a0010478.html

Single Parents: The Lifestyle Magazine for Today's SIngle Parent
http://www.singleparentsmag.com

WEBSITES FOR PARENTS

About.com Single Parents
http://singleparents.about.com/parenting/singleparents/

About.com Stepparenting
www.stepparenting.about.com

Air Force Family Separation and Readiness (tips for visitation for military families)
http://www.afcrossroads.com/famseparation/ret_parent.cfm

Breastfeeding and Visitation Plans
www.lalecheleague.org/NB/NBJanFeb96.law.html

Celebrating Children: Single African American Parenting
http://www.celebratingchildren.com/ . archives-singleparenting.html

Children's Reactions to an Imprisoned Parent
http://www.cwla.org/programs/incarcerated/whathappens.htm

Christian Single Parents Network
http://www.cspn.org

Co-Parenting During Summer Vacation Tips
http://ceinfo.unh.edu/Common/Documents/gsc6600.htm

Coping with Holidays as a Single Parent
http://singleparents.about.com/cs/holidayresources/index.htm?terms=custodial+parent

Directory of Programs Serving Families of Adult Offenders (for the US and Canada: visitation programs for children at prisons)
http://www.nicic.org/pubs/general.htm#new-revised

Discussion Board for Custodial Parents
http://www.mafiaboard.com/wwwboard/

The Effects of Divorce on Children
http://www.hec.ohio%2Dstate.edu/.famlife/divorce/effects.htm

The Electronic Visitation Homepage
http://www3.sympatico.ca/hitechfairdude/yourpage.html

Fathers Are Parents Too
www.fapt.org

Fathers Network
http://www.fathersnetwork.org

Gay and Lesbian Parenting Links
http://singleparents.about.com/cs/gaylesbiparents/index.htm?terms=gay+parenting

Long Distance Families
http://www.longdistancefamilies.com

National Organization of Single Mothers
http://www.singlemothers.org

Parenting Teens
www.parentingteens.com

Parenting Today's Teen: Single Parenting Information
http://www.parentingteens.com/snglpntgarchive.shtml

Prison Family Support Services: Preparing a Child for a Visit
http://www.pfss.org/Preparing.htm

Responsible Single Fathers
www.singlefather.org

Sample Visitation Plans
http://www.familymediationcouncil.com/.publicreading.htm

Single Parent Central
http://www.singleparentcentral.com/.index.htm

Single Parent How To Guide
http://singleparents.about.com/library/blhowtoindex.htm?terms=custodial+parent

Single Parent Tips
http://www.singleparent-tips.com/OurGurus.asp

Single Parents Network
www.singleparentsnetwork.com

Single Parents World
www.parentsworld.com

Single Rose Resource for Single Mothers
www.singlerose.com

Stepfamily Matters
http://www.step-family-matters.20m.com/index.htm

ORGANIZATIONS FOR PARENTS

Academy of Family Mediators
4 Militia Drive
Lexington, MA 02173-4705
781-674-2663
www.mediators.org

African American Family Services (AAFS)
2616 Nicollet Ave., South
Minneapolis, MN 55408
612-871-7878
contact@aafs.net
http://www.aafs.net

Alliance for Non-Custodial Parents' Rights
P.O. Box 788
Inyokern, CA 93527-0788
202-478-1736
www.ancpr.org

American Association of Marriage and Family Therapy
1100 17th Street NW
Washington, D.C. 20036
202-452-0109

American Self-Help Clearinghouse
Northwest Covenant Medical Center
25 Pocono Rd.
Denville, NJ 07834-2995
973-625-3037
ashc@cybernex.net
http://mentalhelp.net/selfhelp

AVANCE Family Support and Education Program, Inc.
National Headquarters
301 South Frio St., Suite 380
San Antonio, TX 78207-4425
210-270-4630
http://www.avance.org

Big Brother Big Sisters of America (BBBSA)
230 N. 13th Street
Philadelphia, PA 19107-1538
215-567-7000
national@bbbsa.org
http://www.bbbsa.org

Bureau of Indian Affairs, Office of Tribal Services
1849 C St., NW, Mail Stop 4660-MIB
Washington, DC 20240
202-208-3463
800-663-5155 (Indian Country Child Abuse Hotline)
http://www.doi.gov/bia/ots/otshome.htm

Center for Child Protection and Family Support
714 G St., SE
Washington, DC 20003
202-544-3144
800-444-6215
ccpfs@centerchildprotection.org
http://www.centerchildprotection.org

Children's Rights Council
300 I Street NE, Suite 401
Washington, D.C. 20002-4389
202-547-6227
www.vix.com/crc/

Coalition for Asian American Children and Families
120 Wall St., 3rd Floor
New York, NY 10005
212-809-4675
cacf@cacf.org
http://www.cacf.org

Committee for Hispanic Children and Families, Inc. (CHCF)
140 W. 22nd St.
Suite 301
New York, NY 10011
212-206-1090
chcfinc@chcfinc.org
http://www.chcfinc.org

Family Support America (formerly Family Resource Coalition of America)
20 N. Wacker Dr., Suite 1100
Chicago, IL 60606
312-338-0900
info@familysupportamerica.org
http://www.familysupportamerica.org

MELD: Programs to Strengthen Families (MELD)
219 North 2nd St., Suite 200
Minneapolis, MN 55401
612-332-7563
info@meld.org
http://www.meld.org

National Association of Custodial Parents
7501 W. Florence Lane
Suite #102
Boise, ID 83704
http://www.cphelp.org/natassn.html

National Center for Missing and Exploited Children (NCMEC)
Charles B. Wang International Children's Building
699 Prince St.
Alexandria, VA 22314-3175
800-THE-LOST
(800-843-5678)
703-274-3900
http://www.missingkids.com

National Child Care Information
Center (NCCIC)
243 Church St., NW
2nd Floor
Vienna, VA 22180
800-616-2242
info@nccic.org
http://www.nccic.org

National Clearinghouse for Alcohol
and Drug Information (NCADI)
P.O. Box 2345
Rockville, MD 20847-2345
301-468-2600
800-729-6686
info@health.org
http://www.health.org

National Clearinghouse on Child
Abuse and Neglect Information
330 C Street, S.W.
Washington, DC 20447
800-FYI-3366
703-385-7565
nccanch@calib.com
http:///www.calib.com/nccanch

National Clearinghouse on Families
& Youth (NCFY)
P.O. Box 13505
Silver Spring, MD 20911-3505
301-608-8098
http://www.ncfy.com

National Congress of
American Indians (NCAI)
1301 Connecticut Ave. NW,
Suite 200
Washington, DC 20036
202-466-7767
http://www.ncai.org

National Congress for Fathers
and Children
PO Box 171675
Kansas City, MO 66117
800-733-3237
http://ncfc.net/ncfc

National Indian Child Welfare
Association (NICWA)
5100 SW Macadam Ave., Suite 300
Portland, OR 97201
503-222-4044
info@nicwa.org
http://www.nicwa.org

National Information Center for
Children and Youth with Disabilities
(NICHCY)
PO Box 1492
Washington, DC 20013-1492
800 695-0285
202 884-8200
nichy@aed.org
http://www.nichcy.org

National Maternal and Child Health
Clearinghouse (NMCHC)
888-ASK-HRSA
(888-275-4772)
http://www.ask.hrsa.gov

National Self-Help Clearinghouse
Graduate School and University
Center of the City University of New
York
365 5th Ave., Suite 3300
New York, NY 10016
212-817-1822
info@selfhelpweb.org
http://www.selfhelpweb.org

Parents Anonymous
675 West Foothill Blvd.
Suite 220
Claremont, CA 91711-3475
909-621-6184
parentsanonymous@
    parentsanonymous.org
http://www.parentsanonymous.org

Parents Without Partners
1650 South Dixie Highway, Suite 510
Boca Raton, FL 33432
561-391-8833
http://www.parentswithout
    partners.org

Single and Custodial Father's Network, Inc.
Fathers Raising Children Project
c/o Goodwill Industries of Pittsburgh
2600 E. Carson St.
Pittsburgh, PA 15203
412-390-2316
http://www.scfn.org/

Single Parents Association
4727 E. Bell Road, Suite 45
PMB 209
Phoenix, AZ 85032
623-581-7445
www.singleparents.org

Stepfamily Foundation
333 West End Ave.
New York, NY 10023
212-877-3244
http://www.stepfamily.org

Stepfamily Association of America
650 J Street, Suite 205
Lincoln, NE 68508
402-477-7837
http://www.saafamilies.org

Supervised Visitation Network
2804 Paran Pointe Drive
Cookeville, TN 38506
931-537-3414
http://www.svnetwork.net

Zero to Three: National Center for Infants, Toddlers and Families
2000 M Street NW, Suite 200
Washington, DC 20036
800 899-4301
202 638-1144
0to3@zerotothree.org
http://www.zerotothree.org

HOTLINES FOR PARENTS

Missing/Abducted Children

Child Find of America
800-I-AM-LOST
(800-426-5678)

Child Find of America - Mediation
800-A-WAY-OUT
(800-292-9688)

Child Quest International Sighting Line
888-818-HOPE
(888-818-4673)

National Center for Missing and Exploited Children
800-THE-LOST
(800-843-5678)

Operation Lookout National Center for Missing Youth
800-LOOKOUT
(800-566-5688)

Family Violence

Family Violence National Domestic Violence Hotline
800-799-SAFE
(800-799-7233)

BOOKS FOR CHILDREN

It's Not Your Fault Koko Bear
by Vicki Lansky

Let's Talk About It: Divorce
by Fred Rogers

Two Homes by Claire Masurel

Mama and Daddy Bear's Divorce
by Cornelia Maude

Why Are We Getting a Divorce?
by Peter Mayle

The Divorce Workbook: A Guide for Kids and Families
Ives, Fassler and Lash

Now I have a Stepparent and It's Kind of Confusing
by Janice S. Stenson

My Parents Still Love Me Even Though They're Getting Divorced
by Lois V. Nightingale

Let's Talk About Living in a Blended Family
by Elizabeth Weitzman

Families are Forever! Kids Workbook for Sharing Feelings About Divorce
by Melissa F. Smith

Don't Fall Apart on Saturdays! The Children's Divorce Survival Book
by Adolph Moser and David Melton

Divorce Happens to the Nicest Kids: A Self-Help Book for Kids
by Michael S. Prokop

Divorced But Still My Parents
by Thomas Shirley

The Suitcase Kid
by Jacqueline Wilson

At Daddy's on Saturday
by Linda Walvoord Girard

The Boy's and Girl's Book About Divorce, With an Introduction for Parents
by Richard Gardner

Can Anyone Fix My Broken Heart? Hope for Children of Divorce
by June Thomas Crews

Dear Daddy by John Schindel

Divorce (Preteen Pressures)
by Debra Goldentyer

Divorce: Young People Caught in the Middle
by Beth Levin

For Better, For Worse: A Guide to Surviving Divorce for Preteens and Their Families
by Janet Bode

Goodbye Daddy
by Brigitte Weninger

How It Feels When Parents Divorce
by Jill Krementz

WEBSITES AND ORGANIZATIONS FOR CHILDREN

Banana Splits (children's divorce support group)
53 Columbus Avenue #2
New York, NY 10023
212-262-4562

Divorced Parents (kids information)
http://member.aol.com/latjan

The Kids Divorce Help Home Page
http://hometown.aol.com/
hypernukls/advice/index.htm

Kids Exchange
http://kidexchange.about.com/
library/weekly/aa012100a.
htm?rnk=r1&terms=
Divorce+Children

BOOKS FOR TEENS

Caught in the Middle: A Teen Guide to Custody
by Claudia Isler

Finding Your Place: A Teen Guide to Life in a Blended Family
by Julie Leibowitz

Help! A Girl's Guide to Divorce and Stepfamilies
from American Girl, The Pleasant Company

It's Not the End of the World
by Judy Blume

Keeping Your Life Together When Your Parents Pull Apart: A Teen's Guide to Divorce
by Angela Elwell Hunt

Money Matters: A Teen Guide to the Economics of Divorce
by Carlienne Frisch

No Easy Answers: A Teen Guide to Why Divorce Happens
by Florence Calhoun

Teens With Single Parents: Why Me?
by Margaret A. Schultz

Understanding the Law: A Teen Guide to Family Court and Minor's Rights
by Anne Bianchi

Why Me? A Teen Guide to Divorce and Your Feelings
by Rachel Aydt

Appendix C

CANADIAN RESOURCES

NOTE: *The resources in this section are specifically for those who are parenting in Canada. If you are in Canada, you should use these resources, but you should also check Appendix B. Most of the books and websites in that appendix are useful for all parents.*

BOOKS FOR PARENTS

Canadian Parents Sourcebook
by Roseman, Darragh

Complete Book of Mother and Baby Care
by Canadian Medical Association

BOOKS FOR CHILDREN

Surviving Your Parents' Divorce: A Guide for Young Canadians
by Michael Cochrane

WEBSITES AND ORGANIZATIONS

Big Brothers and Big Sisters of Canada
3228 South Service Road,
Suite 113E
Burlington, Ontario
L7N 3H8
905-639-0461
800-263-9133
BBSCMaster@aol.com
http://www.bbsc.ca/

Canada Wide Law Pager
http://www.wwlia.org/
   ca-lawof.htm

The Canadian Association for Young Children
http://www.cayc.ca/index2.html

Canadian Association of Family Resource Programs
707 - 331 Cooper Street
Ottawa ON   K2P 0G5
613-237-7667
info@frp.ca
http://www.frp.ca/

Canadian Council for Co-Parenting
613-678-2232

Canadian Mental Health Association
2160 Yonge Street, 3rd Floor
Toronto, ON M4S 2Z3
416-484-7750
national@cmha.ca
http://www.cmha.ca/

Canadian Parents
http://www.canadianparents.com

Canadian Parents Online
http://www.canadianparents.com

**Child CyberSearch
Missing Children Database and Information**
http://www.childcybersearch.org/

Department of Justice (Canada)
http://canada.justice.gc.ca/
Divorce and Defence Strategies (Canada)
416-243-9582
http://www.dadscanada.com

Equal Parents of Canada Mailing List
http://www.interlog.com/%7
Eparental/epocnews/home.htm

Equal Parenting of Durham
http://users.interlinks.net/pmeier/
epd/index.htm

Equitable Child Maintenance and Access Society (Canada)
http://www.ecmas.net
780-988-4015

Family Service Canada
404-383 Parkdale Avenue
Ottawa, ON
K1Y 4R4
613-722-9006
or 800-668-7808
http://www.familyservicecanada.org/
english/mission_frame.htm

Human Equality Action and Resource Team (HEART-Canada)
2 A The Marketplace
East York, ON
M4C 5M1
416-410-4141
http://www.interlog.com/~parental/

Kids Help (Canada): help for children of divorce
800-668-6868
http://kidshelp.sympatico.ca

Legal Information for Canada
http://library.lsuc.on.ca/GL/
home.htm

Men's and Father's Support Groups Across Canada
http://www.canlaw.com/rights/
fathers.htm

Men's Education Support Association (Canada)
Box 4691 Stn C
Calgary, Alberta
T2T 5P1
http://www.mesacanada.com

North America Missing Children Association
http://www.namca.com/english/
english.htm

One Parent Families Association of Canada
http://www.tcn.net/~oneparent

One Parent Families Association of Canada
1099 Kingston Rd. Ste. 222
Pickering, ON
L1V 1B5
905-831-7098
http://hometown.aol.com/opfa222

Ontario StepFamily Association
http://www.angelfire.com/on3/onstep/

Parent and Child Advocacy Coalition (Canada)
http://pcaccanada.tripod.com/

Parent Help Line (Canada)
888-603-9100

Parents Without Partners international number
561-391-3833

Rainbows: an organization that provides peer support groups for children of all ages and adults who are or have experienced divorce
17 Theresa Street
Barrie, ON L4M 1J5
877-403-2733
http://www.rainbows.org

Single Moms in Canada
http://www.topica.com/dir/?cid+2265

Single Parents World (Canada)
http://www.parentsworld.com

Supervised Visitation in Ontario: information and resources
http://www.attorneygeneral.jus.gov.
on.ca/html/FJS/supaccess.htm

> **To Report Child Abuse in Canada:**
> **Kids Help Hotline**
> **800-668-6868**

Appendix D

PHONE NUMBERS FOR REPORTING CHILD ABUSE (STATE BY STATE)

For states not listed, or when the reporting party resides in a different state than the child, call **Childhelp, 800-4-A-Child** (800-422-4453), or your local CPS agency.

Alaska (AK)
800-478-4444

Arizona (AZ)
888-SOS-CHILD
(888-767-2445)

Arkansas (AR)
800-482-5964

Connecticut (CT)
800-842-2288
800-624-5518
(TDD/hearing impaired)

Delaware (DE)
800-292-9582

Florida (FL)
800-96-ABUSE
(800-962-2873)

Illinois (IL)
800-252-2873

Indiana (IN)
800-562-2407

Iowa (IA)
800-362-2178

Kansas (KS)
800-922-5330

Kentucky (KY)
800-752-6200

Maine (ME)
800-452-1999

Maryland (MD)
Call the County Dept. of Social Services or the local law enforcement agency

Massachusetts (MA)
800-792-5200

Michigan (MI)
800-942-4357

Mississippi (MS)
800-222-8000

Missouri (MO)
800-392-3738

Montana (MT)
800-332-6100

Nebraska (NE)
800-652-1999

Nevada (NV)
800-992-5757

New Hampshire (NH)
800-894-5533

New Jersey (NJ)
800-792-8610
800-835-5510
(TDD/hearing impaired)

New Mexico (NM)
800-797-3260

New York (NY)
800-342-3720

North Carolina (NC)
800-662-7030

North Dakota (ND)
800-245-3736

Oklahoma (OK)
800-522-3511

Oregon (OR)
800-854-3508

Pennsylvania (PA)
800-932-0313

Rhode Island (RI)
800-RI-CHILD
(800-742-4453)

Texas (TX)
800-252-5400

Utah (UT)
800-768-9399

Virginia (VA)
800-552-7096

Washington (WA)
800-562-5624

West Virginia (WV)
800-352-6513

Wyoming (WY)
800-457-3659

Index

ABOUT THE AUTHOR

Brette McWhorter Sember is a an attorney and she used to practice in the area of divorce and family law. Her focus was on representing children in custody and divorce cases. As a child advocate, she worked closely with children, visiting them in their homes and schools, going to therapy sessions with them, observing them during visitation and speaking for them in court. She also worked closely with counselors, teachers and social workers as well as with parents.

Ms. Sember is now a full-time writer and has written six other books, which include *How to File for Divorce in New York* and *Child Custody, Visitation and Support in New York*. She writes often about parenting and families for parenting magazines and was a contributor to *Fun Family Activities*. She lives in New York state with her husband and two children.

Visit her web site at **http://www.MooseintheBirdbath.com**.

KOALA!

by Martha Olson Condit

Illustrated by John Hawkinson

SCHOLASTIC BOOK SERVICES

NEW YORK · TORONTO · LONDON · AUCKLAND · SYDNEY · TOKYO

Acknowledgements:

The author wishes to thank Eric Worrell, M.B.E., JP., Director,
Australian Reptile Park, Gosford, Australia, for reading
the text of this book.
A thank you to Mark S. Rich, Curator of Mammals,
Zoological Society of San Diego, California,
for answering many questions.

ISBN 0-590-31996-5
Text Copyright © 1981 by Martha Olson Condit. Illustrations copyright © 1981 by John Hawkinson.
All rights reserved. Published by Scholastic Book Services, a division of Scholastic Inc.

12 11 10 9 8 7 6 5 4 3 2 1   9   1 2 3 4 5 6/8
Printed in the U. S. A.   07

*This book is dedicated
to Milton,
Eleanor, Joan and Jack
and Donna*

Koalas look like cuddly teddy bears.
But they are not bears.
Koalas are marsupials.
That means that when they are babies,
they live inside their mothers' pouches.

koala—say ko-**ah**-luh
marsupial—say mar-**soo**-pee-ull

Night has come to Australia.
Mother Koala sits high up in a gum tree.
She is waiting for her baby to be born.

It is very hot and very quiet.
After a little while, the baby is born.
What a tiny baby—
no bigger than a jelly bean.
His body is pink, and he cannot see.

But he can climb.
He goes through his mother's heavy fur.
He reaches her pouch and crawls in.
Here it is dark and warm.
Little Koala is very hungry.
He gets milk from his mother.
Then he sleeps.

Father Koala is in another tree
guarding three females.
He pays no attention to his new baby.
Soon he will wander away.

It is Mother Koala who cares for Little Koala.
Mother Koala lives in the gum tree.
She sits on a branch
or in a fork of the tree.

It may rain, or the sun may shine.
It may be very windy.
But Mother Koala sits outside,
no matter what the weather.
Her thick fur protects her.

In the daytime, Mother Koala closes her eyes
and sleeps. Once in a while, she wakes up
and nibbles a few leaves.
Sometimes she moves to another branch.
Then she falls asleep again.
At sunset, she is very hungry.
So she looks for lots of leaves to eat.

All this time, Little Koala
just stays in her pouch.
He stays there for about six months.

Mostly Little Koala eats and sleeps
and eats and sleeps.
He is bigger now,
about the size of a tiny kitten.
He can see.
One night he pokes his head
over the edge of the pouch.

After that, he often peeks out.
And now, Little Koala climbs out!
Mother Koala quickly puts her arms
around her baby.

How good the air smells.
For a little while, Mother Koala cuddles him
to her soft body.

Soon, Little Koala is hungry.
Into the pouch he goes
to get milk from his mother.

A few days later, he climbs out again.
Surprise! Surprise!

Mother Koala lets him climb onto her back.
Little Koala snuggles down into her fur.
But not for long.
He begins to look around.
After a short while, into the pouch he goes again.

Every night, Mother Koala must look
for food for herself.
Little Koala rides on her back.

Sometimes a gliding possum comes along.
But Mother Koala is too busy to notice.
She is hungry.
She gets all her food from the gum tree.
She pulls some leaves toward her.

Sniff! Sniff!
Her shiny black nose smells each leaf.
She chooses her leaves carefully.
No. She does not want these.
She moves around the tree.
She reaches for some other leaves.

Sniff! Sniff!
These are good.
She eats the leaves
and even some stems.
In one day she eats enough leaves
to fill a small shopping bag.

When there are blossom buds on the tree,
she eats those too.

In a few months,
Little Koala will be a year old.
He no longer gets milk from his mother.
Instead he drinks a special gum leaf soup
from his mother.

Very soon he is able to eat leaves.
He gets all the water he needs from the leaves.

Now he is too big
to get into his mother's pouch.
But every night he still rides on her back.
She looks for leaves to eat.
But she does not find many in this tree.

Mother Koala is still hungry.
So is Little Koala.
Mother Koala backs slowly down the tree,
down to the ground.
Little Koala holds on.
Mother Koala walks on all fours to another gum tree.

Up she goes with Little Koala on her back.
She finds some good leaves here.
She eats. Little Koala eats too.
Then, Mother Koala falls asleep
with a leaf in her mouth.

All of a sudden, Little Koala jumps
to a branch below.
He wobbles on the branch.
Then he slips. Down, down he falls.

But he grabs a nearby branch and hangs on.
Little Koala squeals. He sounds just like
the squealing brakes of a car.

Mother Koala wakes up.
She backs down the trunk of the tree
to help her baby.
Little Koala twists and pulls himself up
on the branch.

His sharp claws hold him.
Slowly he makes his way to the trunk.
Mother Koala is waiting.
Thank goodness! He is safe.

When Mother Koala can reach him,
she smacks him.
Her baby must learn to be careful.
Little Koala squeals more loudly than ever.
But Mother Koala goes back to her branch.
Back to sleep.

Little Koala crawls onto his mother's back.
For a little while, he whimpers.
Then he falls asleep too.

Little Koala is one year old.
He is as big as a small puppy dog.

Most of the day, Little Koala and his mother
rest in a gum tree.
When it is dark,
Little Koala rides on his mother's back.
Together they go up the trunk of the tree.

Little Koala is ready to climb by himself.
He jumps onto a branch.
This time he does not fall.
Up, up he climbs.

Little Koala's arms and legs are strong.
His claws are sharp.
He can climb up and down trees
all by himself.

But Little Koala still wants to ride
on his mother's back.

One night, he starts to climb on.
Mother Koala stands up.
Push! Push!
She pushes Little Koala away.
He squeals.

But Mother Koala climbs up the tree without him.
Little Koala follows her.
He does not dare to get on her back,
so he sits on a branch below her.

Later, Little Koala jumps over to a nearby tree.
He can still see his mother.
When Mother Koala moves to another tree,
Little Koala moves too.
Sometimes he sits in the same tree.

Now Little Koala is almost two years old.
Mother Koala will soon have another baby.
It is time for Little Koala to find
a home of his own.

Little Koala backs down the tree
to the ground.
From the fork in her tree,
Mother Koala sees him go.

Koalas do not like to walk on the ground.
They are tree animals.
Little Koala ambles along,
looking for a gum tree.
He is hot and tired.
"Yip! Yip!"
What a strange noise.

Suddenly a quick, yellow-brown animal
jumps out of the bushes.
It is a young dingo dog
who has wandered away from his family.

Dingo dogs are wild and fierce and strong.
They are enemies of koalas.
This one is hungry too.

Poor Little Koala!
Dingo Dog circles around him.
Nearer and nearer he comes.
Little Koala runs to a tree.
Dingo Dog runs after him.

Little Koala climbs up the tree,
right to the top.
Here he is safe.
Dingo Dog stands at the bottom of the tree,
yelping at Little Koala.
At last he gives up.
Off he runs.

Little Koala is lucky. He is in a gum tree.
Little Koala eats the leaves.
Now he is tired.
His first adventure
has been an exciting one.
Soon he is sound asleep.

Some Things You May Want to Know about Koalas

In what part of the world do koalas live?

Koalas live in gum tree forests along the eastern coast of Australia.

What is the weather like where koalas live?

It is mostly warm with mild winters and warm to hot summers. Sometimes it can be rainy or very windy.

Summer in Australia begins in December. Autumn begins in March. Winter comes in June and spring comes in September.

How big are koalas?

It depends on what part of Australia they live in. Koalas in the north are smaller than the ones in the south. But, you could say a grown-up koala weighs *about* 9 kilograms (20 pounds) and its body is *about* 62 centimeters long (2 feet).

Are koalas all the same color?

No. Most koalas from the north have yellowish brown fur; those from the middle territory are likely to have gray or grayish fur, while those from the south are usually dark gray or brown, with furry ears.

How many babies are born at one time?

Almost always, only one baby is born at one time.

When are koalas grown-up?

Females are grown-up when they are four years old. Males are grown-up when they are five years old.

How long do koalas live?

Koalas live from 10 to 20 years.

Why do koalas sometimes refuse to eat some leaves on a gum tree?

No one knows for sure. It may be that at different seasons, some of the leaves change and become poisonous for koalas. Perhaps koalas know this and will not eat them. It is possible, too, that as some of the leaves change, they become hard for koalas to digest. Scientists are still trying to find out.

Do koalas ever get sick?

Yes. Koalas may get an eye disease, pneumonia, and other sicknesses. Sometimes they break their legs and arms.

Can koalas swim?

Yes. Koalas are strong swimmers.

Why are koalas such good tree climbers?

Koalas grab the way a person does. When they climb a tree, they use their hands and feet and sharp claws to hold on. There are rough pads on the insides of both hands and feet. These pads help them hold on, too. When they jump, they can land on the pads, which are like cushions.

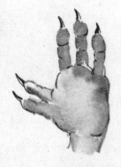

Koalas have two thumbs and three fingers on each hand. At the end of each thumb and each finger, there is a sharp claw.

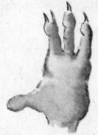

There are five toes on each foot. Except for the first toes, all have sharp claws at the ends. The second and third toes are joined. Sometimes koalas use the claws on these toes to comb their fur.

Do koalas always move slowly?

No. If koalas are scared, they can run fast. They also strike out quickly with their sharp claws.

Do koalas have any enemies?

Yes. The dingo dog, the goanna lizard, and large birds such as the big owl or wedge-tailed eagle are koalas' enemies.

Can anyone have a koala as a pet?

No one is permitted to have a koala as a pet. But a special license to have koalas may be given to a zoo or to a place where scientists keep koalas to learn more about them.

Do people hunt for koalas?

No. Koalas used to be hunted for their fur. But not now. Koalas are protected by the Australian government. No one is allowed to kill them.

Have koalas ever been called by any other name?

Yes. Koalas have been called bangaroo, koolewong, narnagood, buidelbeer, native bear, karbor, cullawine, colo, and gum babies.

How do Australian children help koalas?

Koalas eat only leaves, stems, and blossom buds from gum trees. They do not eat anything else. Australian children plant gum trees so that koalas may have plenty of food.

**SCARLET
HONEYEATER**

Koala's
World

Both the **Gray Kangaroo** and the
Red-necked Wallaby, a member
of the kangaroo family, use
their big hind legs to help them jump.

WALLABY

KANGAROO

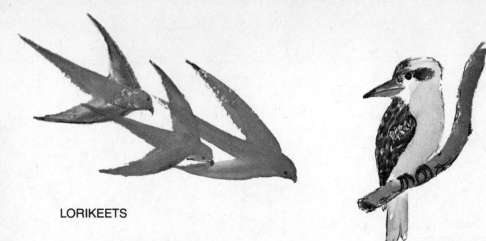

LORIKEETS

KOOKABURRA

The **Common Wombat** lives underground
and comes out at night to eat.

LYREBIRD

With its long sticky tongue,
the **Spiny Anteater** picks up
ants, termites, insects,
and worms.

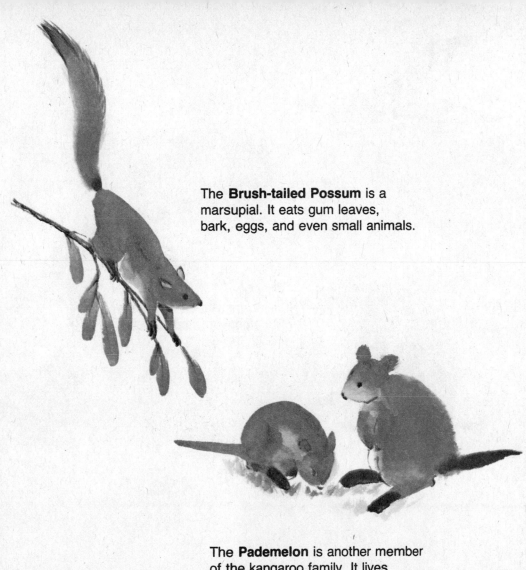

The **Brush-tailed Possum** is a
marsupial. It eats gum leaves,
bark, eggs, and even small animals.

The **Pademelon** is another member
of the kangaroo family. It lives
in tall grass and underbrush.

The **Duck-billed Platypus**
looks for food at the bottom
of a stream.

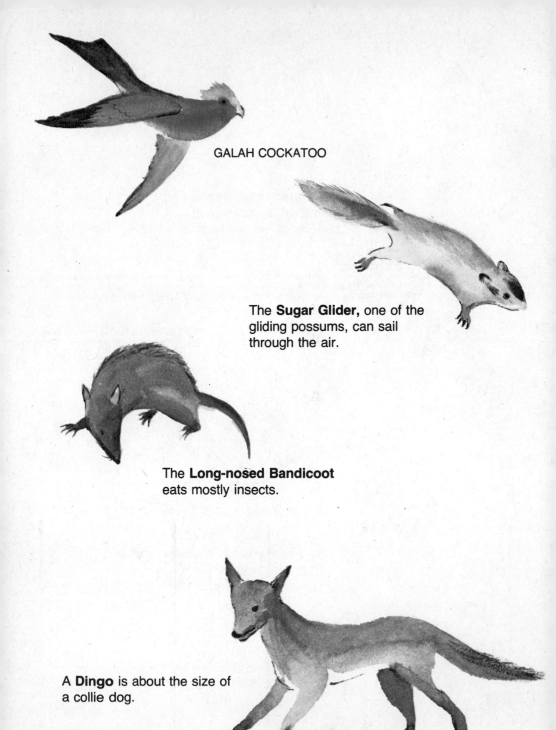

GALAH COCKATOO

The **Sugar Glider,** one of the gliding possums, can sail through the air.

The **Long-nosed Bandicoot** eats mostly insects.

A **Dingo** is about the size of a collie dog.